Fix Your Eyes on Jesus

Fix Your Eyes on Jesus

by

Frank Allred

GRACE PUBLICATIONS TRUST
175 Tower Bridge Road
London SE1 2AII
England
e-mail: AGBCSE@AOL.com

Joint Managing Editors:
T. I. Curnow
D.P. Kingdon MA, BD

First published 2003

ISBN 0 946462-66-8

Distributed by:
EVANGELICAL PRESS
Faverdale North Industrial Estate
Darlington
DL3 OPH
England

Printed and bound in Great Britain by:
Creative Print & Design Wales, Ebbw Vale

Contents

Preface

This book is written in the conviction that the answer to most spiritual problems, both in the Christian church today and in the lives of individual believers, lies in the recovery of an awareness that as the children of God, believers have great privileges. But such recovery is impossible unless we start taking the Bible seriously. Not that the answer to our problems is to be found by becoming more familiar with the text – although it is always a good thing to have an intimate knowledge of the Bible. The answer is to be found rather in the restoration of the vital view of both the Lord Jesus Christ and of the Bible. In spite of all the claims that are currently being made, I am persuaded that there is no other way to regain that heavenly frame of mind which is so vital for our spiritual growth and well-being. Nor is there any other way of stemming the incoming tide of worldliness in the church. I acknowledge the sovereignty of God in the church and in the lives of believers, but this does not relieve us of the duty of fixing our eyes on Jesus – the Jesus of the Bible.

We shall focus in particular on the need to realise afresh our identity as citizens of heaven, who have been called according to God's purpose 'to be conformed to the likeness of his Son' (Romans 8:29), both here and in the glory to come. This world is not our home. We have been called to 'share in the glory of our Lord Jesus Christ' (2 Thessalonians 2:14) in 'a new heaven and a new earth, the home of righteousness' (2 Peter 3: 13). The discipline needed to make progress towards our glorious destiny will be examined.

The main reason why so many believers do not read the Bible or books that promote more in-depth Bible-study, is not primarily, as many claim, that they find them too difficult. With God's help, most of us are capable of much more than we realise. The primary reason is that their preoccupation with the things of this world has made reading and study a low priority. A recent survey revealed that a high percentage of Christian people in England never read their Bibles at all, except perhaps in church on Sundays.

Imagine what would happen if scientists ignored the mass of information handed down to them from former researchers and pioneers. The phenomenal advance in technology over the past two hundred years from stage-coach to space-ship, would not have taken place. Progress would quickly turn to regress, and we would all find life very much more difficult. Every physicist or technician builds on the inherited wealth of knowledge from the previous generation, and he, in turn, hands his knowledge on to the next generation. To do otherwise would be ridiculous. Yet do we not find something like this happening in the church? Is it not true that many believers fail to build on the rich spiritual treasures handed down to us from past generations? And with what result? Our understanding is more limited, our worship more impoverished, our gospel trivialised, our spiritual growth stunted, and our witness largely ineffective. Many dubious trends are seen as exciting new developments when in fact they have all occurred before and have been thoroughly assessed by the great Bible men of the past and roundly rejected.

With few exceptions, visits to Christian bookshops these days confirm this view. Taking the superficial nature of the books on sale as an indicator of the kind of material Christian believers are now interested in, I cease to wonder why so many have no joyful aware- ness of their privileges. Browsing through the shelves of one such bookshop recently, such was the abundance of shallow material, I found it difficult to locate anything of substance that would help believers break out of the superficial mould that now confines so many. The owner of the bookshop told me he doesn't stock works that are more demanding, reprints of works from the great Bible scholars of the past for example, because there is no demand!

Preaching and teaching too suffers the same regress. It has been emptied of biblical content to such an extent that in many places the gospel is hardly recognisable. And the majority of the people who sit in the 'pews' week by week are so lacking in discernment that they are not even aware of the decline. Omissions and deviations from the truth pass unnoticed simply because no-one knows any better.

As a result of this trend, the present generation of believers is likely to go down in history as one of the most biblically illiterate. The principal doctrines of our evangelical faith are but dimly understood. For most believers, the broad sweep of God's purposes in the gospel, from past eternity to its consummation in the coming glory, is unknown. Is it any wonder then that the Christ-centredness that characterised so many of our forebears, is now a rare quality among us? Nor should we be surprised that our sense of security has been undermined, and the quality of our worship and witness adversely affected. When the hope of seeing Jesus in his glory no longer fills our horizon, our incentive to grow into his likeness is bound to grow weak. Indeed, the passion for holiness, which is the fruit of a growing faith that anticipates the glory to come, has cooled to such an extent in our day that our defence against the influence of worldly attitudes and standards has been seriously weakened. A good example of the decline is seen in the ability of believers to put their morals – especially their sexual morals – into a separate compartment from their profession. The number of young people who call themselves Christians and yet commit flagrant breaches of God's moral law without apparently feeling any guilt, has reached alarming proportions. Christians with tender consciences, it seems, are becoming rarer by the day.

During the past fifty years or so there have been several developments, most of them being in the nature of quick fixes, which have been hailed as the solution to the problem. That they have not arrested the spiritual decline is a matter of simple observation. Many writers have applauded the pre-eminence given to the work of the Spirit for example, and see it as a very promising development long overdue. We should all be thankful, they say, that at last teaching on the third Person of the Trinity, neglected for so long, has been restored to its rightful place. Whether or not this is a valid observation will of course depend entirely on whether teaching on the subject is biblical or not. We are deeply grateful for the work of the Holy Spirit in the life of the church. Where would we be without him? He is the one who called us, brought us to repentance and gave us new birth. He is the one who reveals the beauty of Jesus to us, opens the truth of the Scriptures, helps us grow in holiness, and much more. But no departure from Scripture teaching can ever be regarded as a helpful development and, as with any movement in the church, we need to test everything by it. In many churches today, neither the teaching nor the practice would pass the test. Many have gone far beyond what is written (1 Corinthians 4: 6).

The vital question is this: 'Does God the Holy Spirit want pre-eminence?' The Scriptures teach that the task assigned to him is to focus attention on God the Son, because he is the one who reveals the glory of God the Father. The Spirit's work is to bring glory to Christ, and to work in our hearts in such a way that we too will bring glory to him. 'But when he, the Spirit of truth comes' Jesus said, 'he will guide you into all truth. He will not speak on his own; he will speak only what he hears, and he will tell you what is yet to come. He will bring glory to me by taking from what is mine and making it known to you. All that belongs to the Father is mine. That is why I said the Spirit will take from what is mine and make it known to you' (John 16: 13-15). The theme of the Holy Spirit's teaching is Jesus. The Spirit's role is to glorify Jesus. If then we do not exalt Christ, we have no basis on which to claim that the 'blessings' we experience come from the Spirit. And if our testimony causes others to think of the Spirit's work as being in some way separate or superior to that of Christ, we dishonour his name.

It would be wrong, of course, to say that defective teaching on the Holy Spirit is the only reason for the loss of appetite for the word of God and the declining interest in holiness. In many churches not affected by the so-called 'charismatic' movement, hunger for the word of God is rare. Believers are content with 'milk' and have no desire to move on to 'solid food' (1 Corinthians 3: 1). Year after year they remain 'mere infants in Christ' and appear to be content with the situation.

But whatever the cause, the remedy lies in a better understanding of what God has done for us in the Lord Jesus Christ, deepening our appreciation of him and our devotion to him, and strengthening our hope of the glory to come. Far from being a quick fix, this will take time and effort. For many of us it will mean a drastic change in our lifestyle.

Like everyone else, I am a learner in these things. However, I think I am entitled to claim with due humility, that as I grow older, more and more 'wonderful things' are revealed to me in his word (Psalm 119: 18). The brief foretastes of glory the Scriptures have provided have greatly strengthened my desire to know Christ better and to grow in his likeness. If this book promotes that same desire in the hearts of those who read it, I shall be more than satisfied.

Wherever the word 'believers' is used, I am referring to those who believe salvation is by grace alone, through faith alone, by Christ alone, and that the only good deeds acceptable to God are those that are the fruit of faith. Scripture will permit no other definition.

All the quotations from the Bible are from the New International Version unless otherwise stated. Some of the illustrations in the book have been altered, but only enough to protect the identity of the people concerned.

To avoid cumbersome phrases like 'men and women,' 'he or she', and the use of the plural where the singular is preferable, I have used the masculine form. No sex discrimination is intended.

The Glory of Christ

CHAPTER ONE

The Radiance of God's Glory

1. The Glory of God
2. The Radiance of God's Glory
3. The Wisdom of God

*'The Son is the radiance of God's glory and
the exact representation of his being'
(Hebrews 1:3)*

1. The Glory of God

It was Vincenzo Peruzzi who first introduced the 'brilliant' cut – a
method of cutting precious stones to reveal their beauty. A stone cut
in this way has no less than fifty-eight facets, each reflecting light.
Diamonds, especially high quality stones, are particularly attractive
when cut and polished as brilliants. Each facet has a glory of its
own and contributes to the magnificence of the whole. Yet many fail
to see the beauty. When I was in the jewellery trade, it was not
uncommon for a young man, on the point of spending a large sum of
money on a diamond engagement ring, to say – in the presence of
the girl he was hoping to marry – 'It may be a piece of glass for all
I know.' The comment betrays a lack of appreciation, and it is not
very romantic either!

The beauty of Jesus has many facets, each one contributing to
the glory of his Person. In the pages that follow we shall be looking
at just some of those facets in the hope that believing readers will be
more able to appreciate the glory of our Saviour, the Lord Jesus
Christ. We are not surprised that unbelievers do not have eyes to see
any beauty in Jesus, but it comes as something of a shock when we
meet people who claim to be believers but do not appear to discern
his loveliness. What is worse, many of them seem unprepared to

make the effort to improve the situation. What joyful anticipation and sense of purpose we forfeit, if we do not have Jesus and his glory in view!

As a child I struggled with the meaning of the word 'glory,' almost certainly because of the way it was used in common speech. I have vague memories of a fat lady – probably a friend of the family or a relative – whose favourite exclamation when anything went wrong was 'glory be.' When I was older I realised that these two words were taken from the beginning of the doxology, '*Glory be* to the Father, and to the Son, and to the Holy Ghost...' In addition, the tiny room under the stairs at my childhood home where all the junk was kept, and where at least two members of the family would take refuge during the air raids of the Second World War, was called 'the glory hole'. To make matters even worse, we frequently played a game at Christmas in which the old song, 'John Brown's body' figured prominently. The chorus runs, '*Glory, glory*, hallelujah... and his soul goes marching on.' In these circumstances I found it rather difficult to make much sense of the word.

Others may have had an equally confusing introduction, so before we go further we need to be sure what the word really means, especially when used in relation to God in Scripture. Broadly speaking, it is used in two senses. Firstly, it is something that is given to God, as in Luke 2:14: 'the heavenly host appeared with the angel, praising God and saying, "Glory to God in the highest."' Another example occurs in Romans 11:35-36: '"Who has ever given to God, that God should repay him?" For from him and through him and to him are all things. To him be the glory for ever! Amen.' In this sense, the word simply means 'praise' or 'honour'. These two examples are called 'doxologies', a word derived from the two Greek words, *doxa* ('glory') and *logos* ('word'). A doxology is therefore a form of words ascribing praise to God (see also Galatians 1:5 and Ephesians 3:21).

King Herod was eaten by worms – not a very pleasant way to die – because he failed to give the glory to God. After he had delivered a public address to the people, they shouted, 'This is the voice of a god, not of a man.' Immediately, because Herod did not give *praise* to God, an angel of the Lord struck him down, and he was eaten by worms and died. (Acts 12:23; the King James Version translates, 'he gave not God the *glory*').

Secondly, the word is used to describe the being of God, and the excellence of his character as it is revealed in creation, providence and redemption. The word may be used therefore to describe his power, his faithfulness, his exalted position, his perfect will, his presence, his grace, his patience and his love – indeed, all his inherent qualities. In Scripture, the glory of God is described in terms of both light and weight. To young Timothy, Paul describes God as living 'in unapproachable light, whom no one has seen or can see' (1 Timothy 6:16). Probably the apostle had in mind the Old Testament incident when the majesty of God was revealed to Moses (Exodus 33: 18-23). The story illustrates the impossibility of sinful human beings seeing the *full* glory of God. Moses said to the Lord: 'Now show me your glory.' Whether or not Moses knew what he was asking is a moot point, but since he had enjoyed intimate communion with God on Mount Sinai, he could not have been totally ignorant. He was, however, left in no doubt that his request could only be partially granted. 'And the LORD said, "I will cause all my goodness to pass in front of you, and I will proclaim my name, the LORD, in your presence...But...you cannot see my face, for no one may see me and live." Then the LORD said. "There is a place near me where you may stand on a rock. When my glory passes by, I will cover you with my hand until I have passed by. Then I will remove my hand and you will see my back; but my face must not be seen"' We cannot fathom this. Since 'God is spirit' (John 4:24), and therefore has no hands or face, we have to assume that the Lord referred to himself as having bodily parts because Moses would not be able to understand any other way. But the important point is that Moses was protected in some way and was allowed to see no more than his constitution could endure. We may safely conclude, therefore, that the full revelation of the glory of God would be totally overwhelming for any human being.

In terms of 'weight', glory is seen as 'heavyweight' as opposed to what is 'lightweight' and therefore not enduring. Paul, for example, speaks of 'our light and momentary troubles' that 'are achieving for us an eternal glory that outweighs them all' (2 Corinthians 4:17; the King James Version has 'eternal weight of glory'). The apostle sees our present afflictions as light in comparison with the weight of the glory to come. Since the literal meaning of the Hebrew word for 'glory' is 'weight', Paul would, no doubt, have this in mind.

The effect on Daniel of a vision of God sheds further light on the subject. Although he describes his visitor as 'a man', he was obviously no ordinary man. He was 'dressed in linen with a belt of the finest gold around his waist. His body was like chrysolite, his face like lightning, his eyes like flaming torches, his arms and legs like the gleam of burnished bronze, and his voice like the sound of a multitude.' Some would say he was an angel appearing as a man; others a pre-incarnation appearance of Christ, which is much more likely. Calvin says that the 'man' was 'endued, or adorned with attributes which inspire full confidence in his celestial glory.' But whatever view we take, Daniel saw something of God's glory and bowed with his face toward the ground and was speechless. Then, when he recovered his tongue, he said to the one standing before him, 'I am overcome with anguish because of the vision, my lord, and I am helpless. How can I, your servant, talk with you, my lord? My strength is gone and I can hardly breathe' (Daniel 10:5-6, 16-17).

A similar reaction was suffered by Saul of Tarsus and his companions on the road to Damascus. When Jesus appeared in his (partial) glory, the three men travelling with Saul stood speechless; they heard the sound but did not see anyone. Saul himself fell to the ground and was blinded for three days and did not eat or drink anything (Acts 9:1-9).

In texts where the writer is talking about the revelation of God's glory to human understanding, the word 'splendour' is sometimes used and preserves the meaning well. The same idea may be expressed as radiance or effulgence. 'The Son' says the writer to the Hebrews, 'is the radiance of God's glory and the exact representation of his being...' (Hebrews 1:3).

The problem we have in writing about the glory of God is that our limited understanding cannot comprehend it, and the problem is compounded by the inadequacy of language to describe what little we do understand. We cannot therefore avoid putting human limitations on it. It is rather like trying to describe the immensity of the universe. We cannot quantify it; we cannot measure it. Our minds simply cannot cope with it. According to some astronomers, if we started travelling into space at the speed of light – 185,000 miles per second – we would still be passing stars in thirteen thousand million years! The mind boggles. Even so, it would be a serious mistake to jump to the conclusion that we need not try to understand the glory of God. After all, Scripture is written for our learning, not to baffle us. For example, the words of Jesus concerning those whom he has chosen, 'I have given them the glory you gave me,' are recorded for our enlightenment (John 17:22). Likewise, two verses later, when he prays: 'Father, I want those you have given me to be with me where I am, and to see my glory' (John 17:24).

We are, of course, talking about the understanding God gives by faith. Faith always travels further than reason. But this does not mean that faith is sometimes unreasonable. To illustrate the point, when we apply our minds to understand God, we quickly run up against the mystery of the Trinity. We cannot get our minds round the teaching that God is one God in three Persons. But the Trinity is clearly taught in Scripture (even though the word itself is not used) and it is not for nothing that the Scriptures tell us about the function of each Person, and their relationship to each other. Why would God reveal these precious truths to us if we are totally incapable of understanding anything about them? To say that our Triune God is beyond our comprehension does not mean that we must remain ignorant about him altogether. Indeed, if we do not understand something of the task of each Person of the Trinity, we shall never understand the gospel.

The same applies to the glory of God. When it comes to understanding it, the following Trinitarian formula would serve as a simple outline of Scripture teaching: 'The radiance of God the Father's glory is revealed in God the Son and our eyes are opened to his glory by God the Holy Spirit.' Without some understanding of the Trinity, such a statement would make no sense.

We see therefore, that God has revealed himself in his word, not in order that we may *fully* comprehend him, but that our knowledge of him may lead us to give him the glory that is due to his holy name. For this reason alone, every believer should be a serious student of the Bible.

2. The Radiance of God's Glory

The word 'radiance' conveys the idea of an object from which rays of heat or light are emitted. The sun, for example, radiates heat and light. Sometimes the word is used of someone's appearance – an attractive young lady perhaps, who is said to look radiant. In this sense it means she is radiating beauty or glowing with health and happiness.

By calling Jesus 'the radiance of God's glory' (1:3) the writer to the Hebrews is drawing attention to a very precious truth: The incarnate Son is the one from whom the glory of God – his beauty, his holy character, his power and his majesty, his mercy and his justice – radiates. But Jesus is not merely reflecting glory, as a heliograph reflects the rays of the sun. He is the one through whom and *in* whom the glory of God is revealed. Nor is the radiance temporary. The Son was, is, and always will be the radiance of God's glory. Our Lord Jesus Christ is of the very nature of God himself, in all his beauty and majesty.

We believe then, that Jesus is *eternally* glorious as well as being
the radiance of God's glory to us in this *present* time. We are the
privileged ones to whom he is pleased to reveal himself. How can
we fail to rejoice in this? By faith we see his glory in his humiliation
(see chapter three) when he, through whom God created the
universe and now sustains it by his powerful word, became incarnate in order to make purification for our sins (Hebrews 1:3). By
faith we see him who was made a little lower than the angels, crowned
with glory and honour because he suffered death (Hebrews 2:9).

The Lord Jesus Christ is also described in Hebrews 1:3 as 'the
exact representation' of God's being or, as the older versions render
it, 'the express image of his person.' This may give rise to some
questions because we know only too well that God forbids images.
An image is a likeness carved or engraved in metal, wood or stone
or, for that matter, even in the mind. The monarch's head on our
coinage is an image. In what sense then is Jesus the image of God?

Before we try to answer the question we need to remember why
images are forbidden. Because of our sinful pride, we have a
tendency to think we can discover God without his aid. Even when
we have a God-given desire to know more about him, we are still
naturally reluctant to admit that we are altogether powerless to know
what he is like, and therefore need to be constantly reminded that it
is God who reveals himself to us in Christ. If he did not take the
initiative, we would see nothing of his glory at all, and we should
always be quick to admit it. Without God's revelation of himself to
us, our darkened minds would know nothing about him whatever,
and any attempt to visualise him would only bring him down to our
level and keep us in ignorance of him.

For this reason, God is not to be compared to any created being,
for to do so robs him of his glory. 'To whom will you compare me or
count me equal?' asks the LORD, 'To whom will you liken me that
we may be compared?' (Isaiah 46:5). I often think that even the
images of famous people do nothing to enhance their character. For
example, whenever I see the statue of the winged archer in Piccadilly

Circus in London, known as Eros (the Greek god of love) I wonder what it says about the love of the Seventh Earl of Shaftesbury in whose memory it was erected. Why anyone would choose to remember the great man with a statue symbolising erotic love is beyond me. I suppose the authorities could not think of anything more appropriate. If this is the best we can do to portray the character of a man who fought hard for the abolition of the slave trade and for the relief of the poor and underprivileged, what chance have we of portraying the character of God by an image?

I once had a Roman Catholic friend who believed that images are an aid to worship. 'We do not *worship* images;' he insisted, 'we just use them to help us focus our minds on God.' But when I asked him in what way a man-made image can help us worship God who is spirit (John 4:24), he could not answer. God cannot be portrayed by an image for the simple reason that the likeness of what is mortal and created, cannot adequately represent what is eternal and infinite.

There is an amusing story in the Old Testament that vividly illustrates what God thinks about images. The Philistines, the enemies of Israel, captured the Ark of God. The Ark was a gold box containing, along with other things, the Ten Commandments. It was normally placed in the inner sanctuary of the tabernacle where God revealed his will. It served as a symbol (not an image) of the Lord's presence. The Philistines placed the Ark next to their god Dagon in the temple of Dagon. Early next morning, when the people came, presumably to worship their god, they found Dagon flat on his face on the ground. They took him up and probably dusted him down, and put him back in his place. The following morning they found Dagon had fallen flat on his face again, but this time his hands and his head had fallen off. It seems the damage was so severe, poor Dagon could not be repaired! (1 Samuel 5: 1-5).

To return to the question, since images of God are forbidden, even those we carve in our minds, what does Scripture mean when it refers to Christ as 'the image of God' (2 Corinthians 4:4)? How are we to understand this? Does Jesus limit our understanding of God?

If not, why not? The reason is simple; the image of God in Christ is not made by man but revealed by God. It is not carved in wood or stone, but is revealed in the character, the love, and the obedience of the man who is God. So the more we see of Jesus, the more we understand the glory of God. 'For in Christ all the fulness of the Deity lives in bodily form...' (Colossians 2:9). The worshippers of Dagon could gaze at their god for ever and would still be no wiser than the men who made it. But our view of Jesus is never static. When we fix our eyes on him, our view of him grows clearer and brighter all the time.

The writer to the Hebrews wants us to understand that we are specially favoured because God's revelation of himself in Jesus is the culmination of a process that began back in the Old Testament. 'In the past God spoke to our forefathers through the prophets at many times and in various ways, but in these last days he has spoken to us by his Son...' (Hebrews 1:1, 2). Notice the contrasts; God *spoke* in different ways to different people at different times, but now he *has spoken* in one way through one Person at one time. The words 'these last days' do not refer exclusively to the last days of the Old Testament era, but to all the days of the new era, the era that began with the coming of Christ and reaches its climax when he comes again in glory. To put it another way, Christ's first coming marked the beginning of the last days in which we now live. The point the writer is making is this – and we need to take it to heart – that the glory of God now revealed in Jesus is God's final word to this world. God has spoken in his Son, and he will not speak again until the Day of Judgement. The errors that arise from the failure to grasp this principle are neither few nor trivial. The Holy Spirit will, of course, continue to apply the truth of the written word until the day of grace comes to an end.

Although the Son has always been the image of God, it was at his incarnation that he became the representative of God to the world. Had he not taken our nature upon him, we could not have seen the glory of God's grace, mercy and love. It is in Christ as the incarnate

Son, now glorified, that all the excellence of God the Father is seen. This has nothing to do with what Jesus looked like as a human being. Nor does it mean that we see in Jesus the *full* revelation of the glory of God. The apostle Paul acknowledges that 'we see but a poor reflection' and we know only 'in part' (1 Corinthians 13:12). The words 'poor reflection' however, do not mean a 'flawed reflection,' but a dim or limited one. The apostle is comparing what we now see by faith with what we shall see when we are 'face to face' with our beloved Lord in the glory.

In the lounge at my home the main light is controlled by a dimmer switch, which means we can choose the level of brightness. On maximum, the light is too bright for me and I feel the need to turn it down a little. Once turned down, it is the same light, but there isn't quite as much of it. So it is with the glory of God in Christ. He is the 'exact representation' of God's being in the sense that all we can bear to see and all we need to see of the glory of God is revealed in Jesus exactly. To see Jesus is to see God.

Philip, one of the disciples of Jesus, had clearly not understood this when he said to Jesus: 'Lord, show us the Father and that will be enough for us.' Jesus answered, 'Don't you know me Philip, even after I have been among you such a long time? Anyone who has seen me has seen the Father. How can you say, "Show us the Father"? Don't you believe that I am in the Father, and that the Father is in me?' (John 14:8-10).

We too were made in the image and likeness of God (Genesis 1:27) in the sense that we are created as morally responsible and rational beings, crowned with honour and dignity. Although the image remains (James 3:9) it has been grievously marred by sin and its glory has been lost. But Jesus took our mortal nature in all its degradation upon himself – except that he was without sin – so that by his sacrifice for sin we may be 'renewed in knowledge in the image of its Creator' (Colossians 3:10).

What privileged people we are! The joy and the sense of fulfilment of seeing the glory of God 'in the face of Christ' (2 Corinthians

4:6), and being gradually transformed into his likeness until that
day when we shall see him face to face (2 Corinthians 3:18. 1 John
3:2), has no equal on this earth.

3. The Wisdom of God

A friend of mine was both intelligent and knowledgeable. He held a
first class degree from one of the finest universities in the land. But
he lacked wisdom. As a result, he frequently found himself in trouble
for saying or doing the most stupid things. He was the sort of man
you might go to for information, but certainly not for advice.

Wisdom and knowledge, although closely related, are not the
same. A person may lack knowledge but be wise. Another person
may have a great deal of knowledge but still be a fool. After all,
knowledge is nothing more than information in the mind. Wisdom
on the other hand, is knowing how to apply knowledge. It is knowing
what to say and how to behave in any given situation. Knowledge is
theoretical but wisdom is practical. None of us however, no matter
how long we live, or how much learning we do, will ever achieve
perfect wisdom in this life.

How different with God! His knowledge and his wisdom are
infinite. He is able to order all things 'in conformity with the
purpose of his will' (Ephesians 1: 11), so that his perfect plans are
accomplished for his own glory. For those who have eyes to see, his
wisdom and knowledge are clearly seen in creation and redemption.
'The heavens declare the glory of God,' says the Psalmist, 'the skies
proclaim the work of his hands. Day after day they pour forth speech;
night after night they display knowledge. There is no speech or
language where their voice is not heard' (Psalm 19: 1-3). The apostle
Paul too, in the passage we quoted from earlier, is overwhelmed
with gratitude as he contemplates the wonder of salvation: 'Oh, the
depth of the riches of the wisdom and knowledge of God! How
unsearchable his judgments, and his paths beyond tracing out! "Who

has known the mind of the Lord, or who has been his counsellor? Who has ever given to God, that God should repay him?" For from him and through him and to him are all things. To him be the glory for ever! Amen' (Romans 11:33-36).

Human wisdom is acquired through experience of life in this world. It may be put to good use or evil use. An example of its good use is found in Acts 7:22, where Stephen tells us that 'Moses was educated in all the wisdom of the Egyptians and was powerful in speech and action.' Being brought up as the son of Pharaoh's daughter, Moses had the best education Egypt could offer. As the future leader of his people, this would stand him in good stead. The letter of James, on the other hand, speaks of the wisdom that 'is earthly, unspiritual, of the devil' (James 3:15). But whatever purpose is served by human wisdom, we need to understand that it is of no value whatever when it comes to knowing God's way of salvation. In our quest for the knowledge of God, human wisdom must be set aside altogether or it will prove to be a serious hindrance. Why? Because God has decreed that it shall be so. Hear the words of Paul: 'Has not God made foolish the wisdom of the world? For since, in the wisdom of God, the world through its wisdom did not know him, God was pleased through the foolishness of what was preached to save those who believe' (1 Corinthians 1:20, 21). Notice carefully what the apostle is saying. In his wisdom, God has determined that knowledge of him shall not be attained by human wisdom, but by faith in a crucified Christ. To human wisdom, this is ridiculous. How can anyone possibly come to know God through trusting in a crucified man? 'For the message of the cross is foolishness to those who are perishing, but to us who are being saved it is the power of God. For it is written "I will destroy the wisdom of the wise; the intelligence of the intelligent I will frustrate"' (1 Corinthians 1:18, 19).

The only way then to be truly wise, and the only way to increase in godly wisdom – since it is never static – is to fix our eyes on Jesus. He is 'the power of God and the wisdom of God (1 Corinthians 1:24). He is both the focus and the embodiment of divine wisdom and knowledge, for in him 'are hidden all the treasures of wisdom and knowledge' (Colossians 2:3). Paul does not mean that wisdom is so hidden in Christ that it cannot now be found. On the contrary, like gold in a goldmine, it is available to all who are eager to find it. As Matthew Henry comments on this verse: 'The treasures of wisdom are hidden not from us, but for us, in Christ.'

How then are we to acquire this wisdom? We do so by searching the Scriptures, because in them Christ is revealed. Paul's advice to young Timothy is still relevant and needs to be taken to heart: 'But as for you, continue in what you have learned and have become convinced of, because you know those from whom you learned it, and how from infancy you have known the holy Scriptures, which are able to make you wise for salvation through faith in Christ Jesus' (2 Timothy 3:14-16). I realise that many readers will not have had the privilege of a godly upbringing like young Timothy. Nonetheless, if we are to grow in godly wisdom, we simply must become well acquainted with the Scriptures and with the Lord Jesus Christ who is revealed through them. Nowhere else shall we find a greater manifestation of God's power and wisdom. There is no other way to become 'wise for salvation'.

CHAPTER TWO

His Eternal Glory as Redeemer

'And now Father, glorify me in your presence with the glory I had with you before the world began'
(John 17:5.)

1. The Father's Delight

Most of us know what it's like to feel homesick. My worst experience of it was when I was called up at the age of eighteen and found myself trying to cope with the rigours of military discipline. Evidently I was not the only one. After 'lights out' I could hear other young men quietly sobbing as they lay awake. Five years later, when I was enduring the heat and discomfort of the desert and victory over the enemy was in sight, my longing to go home to be with the family was as strong as ever.

Although there can be but little comparison between my experience of being away from home in an unwelcoming land and that of the Lord Jesus coming down from his home in heaven into this sin-sick world, it seems he too wanted to go home. In his prayer to his Father, do we not detect a longing to go back to heaven? When his work on earth was almost done and the victory over sin and death was in sight, he prays these words: 'I have brought you glory on earth by completing the work you gave me to do. And now Father, glorify me in your presence with the glory I had with you before the world began' (John 17:4, 5). His prayer gives us a privileged insight into the desire of his heart, and what, in particular, he now wanted from his Father. As the time of his humiliation draws to a close, he prays for the restoration of his glory, the glory he had with the Father before the world began.

But what is this glory? Many think Jesus is asking for his glory *as God* (the Second Person of the Trinity) to be restored. But this is impossible. His glory as God had never been laid aside. True, it had been veiled during his earthly ministry, but it had never been entirely hidden from view. The man who died on the cross was God incarnate. Christians have always believed this and never stop rejoicing in it. Charles Wesley voiced the convictions of millions when he wrote: 'Amazing love! How can it be that thou my God should'st die for me?'

During the ministry of Jesus this glory shone through his perfect character. It was seen in his love and compassion; in his ability to see into the hearts of people (John 1:48); in his power over nature, and in many other ways. He healed the sick, raised the dead, stilled the storm, and turned water into wine. And yet, in his prayer to his Father recorded by John, he asks for his own glory to be restored, a glory – as the words 'before the world began' clearly show – that was his from eternity.

We also learn from the prayer of Jesus that this glory was *given* to him by his Father (John 17:24). In contrast, his glory as God is the essential quality of all three persons of the Trinity and therefore cannot be given by one Person to another. We do not believe in three gods, but one God in three persons. 'For there is one Person of the Father, another of the Son, and another of the Holy Ghost. But the Godhead of the Father, the Son, and the Holy Ghost, is all one; *the Glory equal*, the Majesty co-eternal' (The Athanasian Creed). How then can the glory of Jesus as God be given to him by his Father?

Furthermore, Jesus reveals the reason why God the Father gave him this personal glory. He refers to it as 'the glory you have given me because you loved me before the foundation of the world' (John 17:24). Now why did the Father love the Son? We do not doubt for a moment that the Father always loved the Son because of the bond of love that must exist between the persons of the Trinity, but Jesus gives us a further reason: 'The reason my Father loves me is that I lay down my life.' (John 10:17). We cannot avoid the conclusion that the Father has a special love for the Son because he was the one who accomplished God's eternal purpose in the redemption of the world. He was the one who suffered the agony of humiliation and death for the sins of his people and for this his Father loved him. It is not easy to get our minds round this, but it is evident nevertheless that it was for the restoration of the glory, a love-gift from his Father back in eternity, that Jesus now prays.

It may come as a surprise to some readers that Jesus should have a glory of his own that is not common to all three persons of the Trinity. But the Scripture teaches that it is so, and both God the Father and God the Holy Spirit are pleased that it should be so. Several texts from both Old and New Testaments speak of the delight the Father takes in his Son as Redeemer. Speaking of Jesus, God says through Isaiah the prophet: 'Here is my servant, whom I uphold, my chosen one in whom I delight. I will put my Spirit on him and he will bring justice to the nations' (Isaiah 42:1). Immediately after the baptism of Jesus, 'heaven was opened... And a voice from heaven said, "This is my Son, whom I love; with him I am well pleased"' (Matthew 3:16, 17). Again, on the Mount of Transfiguration, a voice from the cloud repeated the same words (Matthew 17:5). No doubt it would delight the Saviour's heart as well to hear this expression of the Father's love for him. But they were not merely words of temporary encouragement. On the contrary, they reveal the eternal attitude of the Father to the Son in the context of his amazing sacrifice – an attitude that has never changed and never will. God was delighted with his Son when plans for the redemption of the world were made; he was delighted with him when they were executed; and because his redemption is eternal in its effects, he will be delighted with him forever.

If we may digress for a moment, some readers may wonder whether 1 Corinthians 15:24-28 imposes a time limit on the glory of Christ as Redeemer. At first sight this may seem to be the case. Speaking of the Lord Jesus Christ, the apostle Paul says: 'Then the end will come, when he hands over the kingdom to God the Father after he has destroyed all dominion, authority and power. For he must reign until he has put all his enemies under his feet. The last enemy to be destroyed is death. For he has "put everything under his feet." Now when it says "everything" has been put under him, it is clear that this does not include God himself, who put everything under Christ. When he has done this, then the Son himself will be made subject to him who put everything under him, so that God may be all in all.'

This passage is by no means easy to understand and great care is needed in its interpretation. Perhaps it would be better to clear away some misunderstandings and say firstly what the apostle does *not* mean. When he speaks of Jesus handing over the kingdom to God, Paul is not referring to the kingdom of this world that Christ has both created and redeemed. The new creation in which righteousness prevails belongs to Christ by right and by purchase, and he shall reign over it for ever and ever (Revelation 11:15). Nor does the apostle speak of Christ's rule as Head of the church. He will be Lord of all the redeemed for ever. The only kingdom of which Paul can be thinking is therefore Christ's mediatorial kingdom, the administration of which gives him the power to rule over all those authorities and powers that are his enemies, a rule that will continue until the last enemy is destroyed – which is death itself. The apostle makes it very clear that this aspect of Christ's reign will not end *until* he has put all his enemies under his feet. After this, there will be no point in its continuing because they will all have been put down. His task to put an end to sin and death in all creation will then be accomplished and his authority in this matter will be handed over to God. Jesus himself referred to this authority when he told his disciples just before his ascension into heaven: 'All authority in heaven and on earth has been given to me' (Matthew 28:18). These words indicate that it was an agreement or covenant between the Father and the Son that Jesus should have power to put down all sin and that he should reign until every hostile or indifferent person or institution in the universe has been brought to account. Matthew

Henry, the well-known Bible commentator, says that this mediatorial kingdom is to have an end, 'at least as far as it is concerned in bringing his people safely to glory, and subduing all his and their enemies.'

Many interesting interpretations have been put on the words 'so that God may be all in all' but only one seems to fit the context. When Jesus hands over his authority as Mediator to God, he alone will then be the Sovereign Lord of the universe. But the submission of Jesus to the Father in this matter must not be taken to imply that the Son is not equal to the Father, as some would like to read it. It is Christ as the *incarnate* Son who will be subordinate to the Father and not Christ as the eternal Son. A moment's thought will show that otherwise we would be presented with an absurdity – one of the persons of the eternal Trinity would be downgraded! It is perfectly consistent therefore to say that the Son of God is both equal with the Father (in his eternal nature) and also subject to him (in his assumed nature)! This is indeed beyond our comprehension, but if we rejected all the divine truths that cause the mind to boggle, there would be little left to believe!

How we should rejoice that power in the universe now belongs to Christ until all his enemies and ours are put down. Satan intimidates us; at times evil threatens to overwhelm us and death is our persistent stalker, but our beloved Lord is in absolute control and no power in the universe can touch us except by his consent, and even then the evil powers, not we, are the losers!

To return to the point; the glory the Father is pleased to bestow on his beloved Son as the Redeemer, he is also pleased to bestow upon us, the redeemed. By the grace of God we are privileged to share in his glory in due time, and in the meantime to see his glory by faith. With this privilege comes the ability to understand something of the glory of the Father's love in making an eternal decree to save his elect children from their sins through the sacrifice of his beloved Son. This amazing love is the origin or cause of our redemption, but apart from Jesus we would know nothing of the

Father's loving purposes on our behalf. He is the delight of his Father and he is also our delight. If this does not thrill us to the core, either we have not properly understood the gospel, or we are not believers at all.

2. The Spirit's Delight

We shall examine the role of the Holy Spirit in more detail in chapter five. My purpose here is to show that his delight is to focus attention on the glory of Christ as Redeemer. The teaching of Jesus is unambiguous on this point: 'But when he, the Spirit of truth, comes, he will guide you into all truth' (John 16:13). He is called the 'Spirit of truth' because the truth he reveals concerns Christ and the far-reaching achievements of his death. The Spirit's task is not to speak on any or every subject, but to reveal truth about the redemption accomplished by the Lord Jesus.

The promise therefore, that the Holy Spirit will lead us into '*all* the truth,' (literal translation) means that he reveals everything we need to know about redemption. Because all the various aspects of redemption truth hang together, it will help us if we think of them as a *body* of truth revealed in Holy Scripture. The Spirit does not go off at a tangent and start revealing new things about our redemption. Nor does he emphasise one aspect of truth at the expense of the others. Nor, for that matter, does he interpret Scripture in one way to one person and in another way to someone else. This may seem obvious to many readers, but for others apparently it is not so obvious. We cannot deny that in the church today it has become fashionable to have a pet theory about the work of the Spirit. We need to understand as a matter of urgency that the Spirit is never the originator of either error or imbalance.

In this connection it is also important to understand that the Spirit does not act on his own. Jesus goes on to say, 'He will not speak on his own; he will speak only what he hears' (John 16:13). This is exactly what Jesus said about himself: '...I do nothing on my own but speak just what the Father has taught me' (John 8:28). We see then that the Son and the Spirit both say the same thing, and both say what the Father has told them to say. If only this unity of purpose in the Trinity could be firmly grasped by the church, we would avoid a thousands pitfalls. As things stand, we are not nearly as careful as we should be in recognising that the Spirit's delight is to glorify Christ as Redeemer according to the will of the Father. The practice of glorifying the Spirit, now common in many churches, can only be seen as a grievous misunderstanding of the function of the persons of the Trinity. The third verse of a song that has become rather popular in recent years will serve as an example of the trend:

> Spirit, we love You,
> we worship and adore You:
> glorify Your name in all the earth.
> *Donna Adkins*

No doubt the author's intentions were good, but it is still wrong to ask the Spirit to glorify himself in the earth. It is asking the Spirit to do something that runs contrary to his ministry. His delight is not to glorify himself, but Christ.

3. The Son's Accomplishment

We should not think it strange then, in view of the redemption that Christ has accomplished, that both God the Father and God the Holy Spirit are pleased that God the Son should have the supremacy. Even in human enterprises where father and son are concerned, the father is usually content that his son should be pre-eminent. When, for example, father and son set up a business and call it 'Thomas Smith and Son,' it is immediately apparent that although father and son are working together in harmony for the success of the enterprise, the father is content that his son should not only play a prominent role, but eventually inherit the company with all its assets. No doubt Tom Smith would make a will to this effect.

What is different about the agreement between the Father and the Son however is that the Son has always been at the centre of his Father's plans. According to these eternal plans, Jesus as God incarnate is the one who redeemed the universe, and he is the one who will inherit it. That it should be so is the Father's unchangeable will. For Christ created all things 'in heaven and on earth, visible and invisible, whether thrones or powers or rulers or authorities; all things were created by him and for him. He is before all things, and in him all things hold together. And he is the head of the body, the church; he is the beginning and the firstborn from among the dead, so that in everything he might have the supremacy. For God was pleased to have all his fulness dwell in him, and through him to reconcile to himself all things, whether things on earth or things in heaven, by making peace through his blood, shed on the cross' (Colossians 1:16-20).

We shall look in a little more detail at the glory of a redeemed universe in chapter twelve. The point to be emphasised here is that our future glory is the fruit of Christ's redemption, and has been accomplished once and forever on Calvary's cross. And it is important to understand, before we go further, what an amazing thing it is that we redeemed sinners are privileged to see that glory by faith here and now. It was first revealed to the apostles by the Spirit, and through their writings by the same Spirit to us! For to the apostles, God made known 'the mystery of his will according to his good pleasure, which he purposed in Christ, to be put into effect when the times will have reached their fulfilment – to bring all things in heaven and on earth together under one head, even Christ' (Ephesians 1:9, 10). Here Paul first looks back to the 'time' before the foundation of the world, when the plan of redemption was drawn up, and then on to the end of time when its fulfilment will be seen in the coming together of the redeemed church and the renewed universe. This must surely have something to do with the glory Jesus had with the Father that we spoke about earlier – the glory he had as the Redeemer of the world even before it was created. No other conclusion is possible.

Where then do we come in to this scheme of things? Remember the prayer of Jesus to his Father: 'I want those you have given me to be with me where I am, and to see my glory, the glory you have given me because you loved me before the creation of the world' (John 17:24). In the mercy of God we are 'given' to the Lord Jesus, and thrilled that it should be so. He has bought us with his own blood, and the Holy Spirit has been given to us as 'a deposit guaranteeing our inheritance until the redemption of those who are God's possession – to the praise of his glory' (Ephesians 1:14). In passing we should notice that the word 'redemption' is used in a different way in this verse. Sometimes it means *past* deliverance from the penalty of sin, and sometimes *future* deliverance from all that is evil and corrupt. Obviously the latter meaning applies here because Paul is looking forward to the day of our final deliverance.

Our view of the glory of that great day of redemption, opened up to us by the Spirit through the Scriptures, gives solid ground for comfort in the present, and courage and confidence for the future. We are able to rejoice that Jesus is Lord of the visible world, Lord of the invisible world, Lord of the Church, and the inheritor of everything. Unlike Tom Smith's plans for his son, which are made in time and will end in time, God's plan to glorify his Son was made in eternity and his glory will never end. It is the glory we shall share. What spiritual paupers we are if we know nothing of the glory of Christ the Redeemer! It is a solemn thought that only those who see his glory as Redeemer in this life by faith will partake of his glory in the future.

CHAPTER THREE

The Glory of His Humiliation

1. The Glory of His Incarnation
2. The Glory of His Obedience
3. The Glory of His Cross
4. The Believer's Boast

'The Word became flesh and made his dwelling among us. We have seen his glory, the glory of the one and only Son, who came from the Father, full of grace and truth.
(John 1:14).

1. The Glory of His Incarnation

Charles Wesley's well-known hymn: *'And can it be that I should gain an interest in the Saviour's blood?'* to which we have already referred, was sung fairly frequently in the chapel of the college where I trained for the ministry. It was good to hear about sixty theological students singing heartily. But without fail, every time we reached the third line of the following verse, most of the men stopped singing. But why?

> He left his Father's throne above –
> so free, so infinite his grace –
> *emptied himself of all but love*
> and bled for Adam's helpless race.

In some older versions of the Bible, the words 'made himself nothing' (Philippians 2:7) are translated, 'emptied himself.' The two words have been the cause of much debate and disagreement down the years. The argument has centred on the question, 'of what did Jesus empty himself?' Being fully God and fully man, he certainly did not empty himself of his deity. That is to say, the incarnation did not change the nature of Jesus as God, although the glory of his deity must have been veiled to some extent. This was the main reason why the students did not feel able to sing the offending line. Our purpose here is not to go into the detail of the argument, but just to pose the question: What glory do we see in the incarnation, life and death of Jesus and to what extent is it revealed?

Up to a point, the question has already been answered. Jesus is 'the radiance of God's glory and the exact representation of his being' (Hebrews 1:3). We do not hesitate therefore, to repeat our assertion that the incarnate Son is the most glorious revelation of the love, grace, mercy, and holiness of God it is possible to see. Nowhere else and in no one else are these attributes of God so finely displayed. By taking our nature upon him, Jesus became the one in whom the very nature of the invisible God becomes visible (Colossians 1:15).

We see the glory of Jesus revealed even *before* he was born. The forthcoming event was announced to the Virgin Mary by the angel Gabriel, who told her that 'The Holy Spirit will come upon you, and the power of the Most High will overshadow you. So the holy one to be born will be called the Son of God' (Luke 1:35). The angel's words explain how Jesus was born without a tendency to sin. The natural process whereby this tendency is passed from parents to children was set aside by the power of God. Had Jesus been born in the natural way, he would have had a sinful nature just as we do. In the event however, 'the power of the Most High' ensured that Jesus did not inherit such a nature from his mother, even though she was not without sin; nor could he inherit it from Joseph, his human 'father,' because he had nothing to do with it. Only by 'the power of the Most High' could 'the Son of God,' 'the holy one,' be born without sin.

It is also important to understand that Jesus did not *begin* to be the Son of God from his birth. He was always the Son of God, the difference now being that as a result of his supernatural conception,

he is revealed in human form as the Son of God. The words of the
angel also show that being born of a woman, Jesus was truly
human. He could not be our Saviour unless he became a human
being like us, as well as being free from every taint of sin. Truly, the
glory of God is revealed in the virgin birth, and only those who are
blind to it, will try to deny it.

How Jesus can be born wholly God (being infinite and eternal)
and wholly man (being finite and having a beginning in our world)
is beyond our comprehension. But this is no reason for denying it. If
it were, we would have to deny the resurrection as well because we
can't understand that either. 'Nothing is impossible with God' (Luke
1:37) – and we should readily acknowledge that there is always an
incomprehensible element in divine revelation. Like everything else
the Bible reveals, the glory of the Person of Christ Jesus as both
God and man is perceived only by faith. It is impossible for those
without faith to see any glory in him at all.

From time to time Jesus revealed his divine glory to those men
who were privileged to be his chosen disciples. On one occasion,
thirty years after his birth, Jesus performed an astonishing miracle
of turning water into wine. Along with his disciples, he was invited
to a wedding, and for some reason, the wine ran out. The mother of
Jesus, who was also present, reported the embarrassing circumstances
to him. In obedience to his command, the servants filled six huge
water-jars to the brim with water and served it to the guests. Somewhere in the process, the water had been turned into such good wine
that the master of ceremonies commented on it. But the apostle John,
who relates the story (John 2:1-11), gives us the surprising information that apart from the servants, only the disciples knew what had
happened. 'This,' says John, was 'the first of his miraculous signs,
Jesus performed in Cana of Galilee. He thus revealed his glory, and
his disciples put their faith in him' (Verse 11).

Clearly then, for the apostle John and the other disciples, this
'first' miracle revealed yet more of the glory of Christ and led to an
increase in their faith. Through the miraculous event, the veil over

Christ's creative power and majesty was drawn aside, giving the disciples a brief glimpse of his divine glory. No doubt, the same was true of the other miracles John records, like the feeding of the five thousand (John 6:1-15), Jesus walking on water (John 6:16-21), and the raising of Lazarus from the dead (John 11:1-44).

The glory of Christ's humiliation is brought into even sharper focus for us when we see his care and compassion for ordinary people, especially his disciples and his friends. This caring love is summed up in the Lord's own words, spoken to his disciples when a recurring dispute (see Luke 9:46) arose among them as to which one of them was considered to be greatest. 'But I am among you as one who serves' Jesus said (Luke 22:27). The contrast between his power and majesty on the one hand, and his condescending love on the other, was graphically demonstrated on the occasion when Jesus washed his disciples' feet. The small party had just arrived in the upper room from the town of Bethany. Because only sandals were worn, and the roads were dusty, it was customary for the host to ensure that a servant was available to wash the feet of guests as they arrived. Since no such service was available on this occasion, it would have been appropriate for one of the disciples to perform the menial task. It seems they were all too proud. And so it was that these men, who had been privileged to have glimpses of Christ's power and glory, now watched him get up from the meal, take off his outer clothing, wrap a towel around his waist, and wash their feet! (John 13:2-5).

The glory of Jesus is also seen in the truth that it is he, *as man*, who fulfils God's purpose for men. God created man in his own image and gave him rule over all things (Genesis 1:26, 28), but on account of sin he failed to realise God's purpose. But now, the man Christ Jesus, who is our representative, has achieved it on our behalf. He has been found worthy to be ruler over all things. Not only that, but by his suffering and death on our behalf, we too have been made worthy of restoration to the glory of that honoured position. Our restoration is not yet obvious, but the eye of faith already sees Jesus crowned with glory and honour, and he is the guarantee that God's purposes for mankind will be accomplished. The writer to the Hebrews expresses it like this: 'It is not to angels that he (God) has subjected the world to come, about which we are speaking. But there is a place where someone has testified: "What is man that you are mindful of him, the son of man that you care for him? You made him a little lower than the angels; you crowned him with glory and honour and put everything under his feet." In putting everything under him, God left nothing that is not subject to him. Yet at present we do not see everything subject to him. But we see Jesus, who was made a little lower than the angels, now crowned with glory and honour because he suffered death, so that by the grace of God he might taste death for everyone' (Hebrews 2:5-9. Psalm 8).

For believers then, the man who was born of the virgin is the one who has fulfilled God's purpose on our behalf. As perfect man, he is the one who has restored us to the honoured place intended for us, as men. He is the one who reveals the Father to us, and shows us what we should be like as human beings in preparation for the day when we shall take our honoured place. He is the one who has gone back to heaven to prepare that place for us. To achieve all this it was necessary for him, as a man, to live for a while among us (Philippians 2:8; John 1:14); to enter into our sufferings and to be familiar with our deepest griefs and fiercest trials (Isaiah 53:3). He therefore is the one on whom, by faith, we fix our eyes.

We must not settle for any teaching that denies either his divinity or his humanity. During the course of history the teaching that Jesus is both fully human and fully divine has frequently been under attack. Various perversions of the truth have threatened the church from time to time – the idea for example that Jesus is half human and half divine, or just an ordinary man into whom the Spirit of God came in a special way. Nor must we give the slightest impression that since the Son became incarnate, he is in some way eternally inferior to the Father or the Spirit. It is true of course that as a man, in his role as Mediator, he willingly took a lower position. This is what Jesus meant when he said: 'the Father is greater than I' (John 14:28). The Jehovah's witnesses are very fond of quoting this text to 'prove' that Jesus is a created being, but they do not understand (or are not prepared to accept) that Christ's inferior position was entirely voluntary, and that in essence he is equal to the Father (Philippians 2:6).

It was precisely because of his willingness to step down from his throne and become obedient to death, that God has given him 'the name that is above every name, that at the name of Jesus every knee should bow, in heaven and on earth and under the earth, and every tongue confess that Jesus Christ is Lord to the glory of God the Father' (Philippians 2:9-11). The Father has determined that Christ shall 'have the supremacy' (Colossians 1:18). 'Moreover, the Father judges no one, but has entrusted all judgement to the Son, that all may honour the Son just as they honour the Father. He who does not honour the Son does not honour the Father, who sent him' (John 5:22, 23). Jesus has the highest honour.

How brightly then the glory of Jesus shines in his incarnation for all who have eyes to see! We are assured that he was made flesh, in our likeness, so that we who are given to him by the Father, may one day be made in his likeness! All who are so persuaded would not surrender their view of the glory of the incarnate Son for all the world.

But seeing God's glory in the virgin birth is not quite the same as seeing it in the poverty, suffering, and death of Jesus. The virgin birth is a cause of wonder and amazement because it is miraculous. But there is nothing miraculous about his poverty, his temptations, and especially his death – only humiliation. After all, glory and humiliation are opposites. If a king divests himself of his royal robes, steps down from his throne, goes to live with the lowest of the low, suffers untold agonies and dies an ignominious death, in what sense can he be said to be revealing his majesty? And what Jesus did was much more humiliating than this. As a perfect man he suffered untold agonies in this dark and sin-sick world; he endured the frailty of our humanity; and he exposed himself to physical weariness, pain, hunger, and thirst. He willingly became the subject of the severest of Satan's temptations, and finally endured the cross and suffered the agony of separation from his Father. We may speak of the indignity suffered by kings who lose their thrones, of the shame of rich people who lose their wealth, but nothing compares with the voluntary suffering of the one who, 'though he was rich, yet for your sakes he became poor, so that you through his poverty might become rich' (2 Corinthians 8:9).

Yet, although the New Testament preserves the distinction between the humiliation of Christ's condescension and the glory of his resurrection and exaltation, it also reveals the glory of his humiliation. The Gospel of John and the letters of Paul in particular focus on it. It is not so prominent in the Gospels of Matthew, Mark and Luke, but even there it is revealed to some extent. Many examples could be given. The glory of the love of Jesus is displayed in his willingness to take our flesh in order 'to save his people from their sins' (Matthew 1:21). The excellence of his character is seen in the way he confronts the fierce temptations of the devil (Matthew 4; Luke 4); and also in his single-minded dedication as he sets his face towards Jerusalem, knowing full well what would happen to him there (Mark 10:32-34).

But much more is revealed in the writings of the apostles John and Paul. They focus on the glory of Christ's submission to his Father's will in order to achieve the redemption of the elect, and on the glory of his perfect obedience to his Father's commandments which was necessary for its accomplishment. And not least, they focus on the glory of the cross.

2. The Glory of His Obedience

My mother ran a wool shop. One day, still vivid in my memory, she caught me with my hand in the till. I can still hear the stern but sad tone in her voice: 'Did God tell you to do that?' she demanded. The answer to the question was not difficult, but feeling ashamed, I remained silent. After seventy years the shame is still with me. My father's disapproval of my habitually bad behaviour also comes to my mind readily. His repeated question still rings in my ears: 'Why can't you do what you are told?' This was a much harder question and at that time I would have had no idea how to answer it. I didn't know why I behaved so badly; nor was I particularly interested in finding out. My dad was not, of course, expecting an answer. At that age, words like 'obedience' and 'discipline' were unpleasant to my ears and tended to aggravate my rebellious spirit. They sounded threatening and restrictive. It was not that I did not *want* to honour my parents, but I enjoyed doing the things I was not supposed to do – at least until the time of reckoning came. And even then, the effect of the scolding didn't last long. The idea of anyone being *pleased* to do what they are told was difficult for me to take in.

Later on, against this background, the claims of Jesus made a deep impression on me. Throughout his earthly life he was *pleased* to obey his Father perfectly. And what was his motive? 'The world must learn' Jesus said, 'that I love the Father and that I do exactly what my Father has commanded me' (John 14:31). And again in John 15:10: 'If you obey my commands, you will remain in my love, just as I have obeyed my Father's commandments and remain in his love.' I loved *my* father too, but not like this. No other human being has ever done so either. And therefore none has been able to give perfect obedience. If we see no glory here, we are blind indeed.

In my early years, as I have just described, I wanted to be free of rules and orders. But like everyone else born into this world, I had no choice in the matter. How different it was with Jesus who deliberately chose to be under the law! He who was above the law was willing to be born under the law. He was willing to obey the law *before* he was obliged to obey it. He came into the world with the very purpose of doing the will of his Father. 'Therefore, when Christ came into the world, … he said, "I have come to do your will, O

God"' (Hebrews 10:5-7). And this first act of obedience characterised his entire life.

But why did he choose to be born under law? Was it just to
demonstrate that he, as a human being, could keep it? Such an exhibition might serve as an example to us but it would do nothing to save
us from our sins. No, he chose to keep the law so that he could offer
his perfect life in sacrifice to clear the guilt of those who were under
obligation to keep the law, but failed to do so. 'For just as through
the disobedience of the one man the many were made
sinners, so also through the obedience of the one man the many will
be made righteous' (Romans 5:19). Paul is not teaching that by
believing in Christ we immediately become *perfectly* righteous in all
we do. He is saying that God reckons the righteousness of Christ as
ours, just as he regards the disobedience of Adam as the disobedience of all who do not believe. In Adam many are declared sinners;
in Christ many are pronounced righteous. Or again, when the apostle
says: 'God made him who had no sin to be sin for us, so that in him
we might become the righteousness of God' (2 Corinthians 5:21),
he means that the perfect Son of God was regarded and treated as a
sinner so that we sinners may be regarded and treated as righteous,
and on that basis welcomed into God's family. 'God sent his Son,
born of a woman, born under law, to redeem those under law, that
we might receive the full rights of sons' (Galatians 4:4, 5)

How precious is Jesus! He is the spotless lamb of God without
blemish or defect (1 Peter 1:19); and how privileged we are to be
able to see beyond the endless innuendos and insinuations about his
character made by unbelievers, to the glory of his sinless life. When
Jesus laid down the challenge to the Jews: 'Can any of you prove me
guilty of sin?' (John 8:46) there was nothing they could say, even
though they had been watching him carefully. (For any other human
being to say this would be seen as insufferable arrogance, and it
would not be difficult to rise to the challenge.) And yet, even though
they were so close to him, they saw no glory in him. But the privilege of seeing his glory is granted to us so that we may make use of

it. It is given to us as God's elect children, not only that we may appreciate the completeness of our salvation, but also that we may contemplate his perfection as a human being and follow in his steps (1 Peter 2:21-23).

The glory of Christ's obedience is intensified by his compassion. There is nothing very attractive about people who are law-abiding but cold. If given the choice, most of us would prefer a warm-hearted rascal to a cold-hearted saint. But Jesus was not only a righteous man (Luke 23:47), but also a good man (Romans 5:7) – one who was warm-hearted and kind, willing to go the second mile (Matthew 5:41). For him, the path of obedience was also the path of suffering, and as a result we have a high priest who is able to sympathise with our weaknesses; one who has been tempted in every way, just as we are – yet was without sin (Hebrews 4:15).

3. The Glory of His Cross

The regimental badge of the 17th Lancers, designed in memory of General Wolfe, depicts a skull with the words 'or glory.' As a result, the soldiers who belonged to the regiment were known as 'the death or glory boys.' The designer obviously thought of death and glory as opposites – soldiers either gain glory on the battlefield, or die. It is a rather tragic concept, because as a rule, glory or no glory, soldiers don't want to die. And even if they gain glory (*and* die), it is soon forgotten. Although those who perished fighting for their country are described as 'Our Glorious Dead,' most people see more sadness than glory in it.

How different it is with the death of Jesus! Believers are enthralled by the glory of it, and have been for two thousand years. His life was not 'lost' in pursuit of victory, but was freely given to achieve it. His death *itself* is victory – victory over Satan, over sin, and over death. The words of Jesus from the cross just before he 'gave up his spirit' are not words of defeat, but of triumph: 'It is finished' (John 19:30). The victory was won; the work of redemption was done. Jesus had kept the law of God perfectly, and had borne the penalty for breaking it on behalf of all his people. What can be more glorious than this?

In one church in which I served I always found myself in trouble on Good Friday because I would not allow black drapes to be placed over the cross. The people who complained defended the practice by insisting it was 'the tradition of the church.' 'What right have you, they demanded, 'to abolish a long-standing tradition?' But when I asked them to tell me why Good Friday should be a day of mourning, all they could say was, 'It was the day Jesus died.' The glorious things he accomplished by his death didn't appear to come into their reckoning.

John draws our attention to some words of Jesus himself – words that tend to prove that he saw the hour of his death as an exhibition of his glory. In reply to the request of some Greeks who wanted to see him, Jesus said: 'The hour has come for the Son of Man to be glorified' (John 12:23). Again, after Judas the traitor had left, Jesus said to his disciples: 'Now is the Son of Man glorified and God is glorified in him. If God is glorified in him, then God will glorify the Son in himself, and will glorify him at once' (John 13:31, 32). Some take the view that Jesus was referring exclusively to the glory that followed his sacrifice, but if that were the case, why would Jesus identify his glory so closely with his imminent death? Is it not much more likely that his words focus on 'the hour' or 'the time' that up to this point had been described as 'not yet come' (John 7:30; 8:20)? And since the Father is glorified *in* his Son in this hour, how can his words refer to anything other that the glory of his death? What an inexplicable omission it would be if John just passed over the glory of Christ in being willing to die for the sins of the world, to say nothing of the glory of his Father in giving up his Son for this purpose? Certainly this is what we, his redeemed people, admire so much. This is the reason we glorify God. And think also of the glory of God's love and justice; the glory of his faithfulness and power, demonstrated in the cross! Bishop Ryle (1816-1900) suggests that John 13:31, 32 (above) may probably be paraphrased as follows:

'Now has the time come that I, the Son of Man, should be glorified, by actually dying as man's substitute, and shedding my blood for the sins of the world. Now has the time come that God the Father should receive the highest glory by my sacrifice on the cross' (*Expository Thoughts on the Gospels.*)

Not only John, but Paul too insists that the cross is an exhibition of the glory of God. He tells us that not only has he 'cancelled the written code, with its regulations, that was against us' by 'nailing it to the cross,' but he has also 'disarmed the powers and authorities' and 'made a public spectacle of them, triumphing over them by the cross' (Colossians 2:14, 15). In other words, by the death of his Son, not only has God cancelled all our debts but has also vanquished the powers of hell and exhibited them to public shame – like a conqueror returning from the battle in glorious triumph leading a procession of defeated captives.

According to Paul the cross is also demonstration of the justice of God: 'God presented him as a sacrifice of atonement' ('the one who would turn aside God's wrath' is better) 'through faith in his blood. He did this to demonstrate his justice … at the present time, so as to be just and the one who justifies those who have faith in Jesus' (Romans 3:25, 26). God's justice in justifying sinners is made known to us in the death of Christ, and nowhere else. Because the perfect sacrifice he offered on our behalf is acceptable to God, justice has been done and we are free.

But not only his justice, for Paul goes on to say that the cross displays God's love too:'God demonstrates his own love for us in this: While we were still sinners, Christ died for us' (Romans 5:8). What love we see in his willingness to humble himself so that we may be exalted! And nowhere else is that love so conspicuously displayed as in the cross.

> My song is love unknown, my Saviour's love to me;
> Love to the loveless shown, that they might lovely be.
> O who am I, that for my sake
> My Lord should take frail flesh, and die?
> *Samuel Crossman c1624-83.*

John goes further: 'This is how we know what love is: Jesus Christ laid down his life for us' (1 John 3:16). Here the apostle maintains that the cross reveals the farthest extent to which love will go, and therefore the revelation of what love really is. Not only the truth *about* God's love is revealed, but also the *nature* of it. He 'so loved the world that he gave his one and only Son...' (John 3:16).

The wisdom and the power of God in our salvation are also revealed in the death of Christ, exposing the bankruptcy of the wisdom of this world. As a child I was taught a well-known rhyme. I think it was supposed to help me understand the importance of keeping my mouth shut – (a parallel with that other doubtful but well known maxim, 'children should be seen and not heard'):

> The wise old owl sat on an oak;
> the more he saw, the less he spoke.
> The less he spoke, the more he heard;
> wasn't he a wise old bird?

If the rhyme is intended to define wisdom, it simply will not do, for if the old owl didn't do anything with all the knowledge he acquired, how could he possibly be wise? Wisdom, according to the dictionary, is not just learning, but 'the ability to make the right use of knowledge.' What use is knowledge if we don't know how to use it?

When it comes to the wisdom of God revealed in the death of Christ however, the dictionary definition is not good enough. It leaves open the question as to how the knowledge and the ability to make use of it, are acquired. The knowledge of salvation is certainly not something we learn by keeping our eyes open and our mouths shut like the old owl; it is revealed by God to the eye of faith. And the ability to make the right use of that knowledge is not something we gain with experience alone; it is the power of God at work in us. To all whom God calls, God reveals and *imparts* wisdom and power. Both are God's gifts. '... to those whom God has called, both Jews and Greeks, Christ the power of God and the wisdom of God' (1 Corinthians 1:24). He has given us the precious gift of faith so that we may not only have the knowledge of salvation, but also the wisdom to know how to use it. That is to say, by the grace of God we are now able to apply the knowledge of God to the matter of daily living, in holiness and righteousness. In Paul's words, we 'are in Christ Jesus, who has become for us wisdom from God – that is, our righteousness, holiness and redemption' (1 Corinthians 1:30).

But there is yet more to the wisdom of God revealed in the cross. A crucified Christ is 'a stumbling-block to Jews and foolishness to Gentiles, but to those whom God has called, both Jews and Greeks, Christ the power of God and the wisdom of God' (1 Corinthians 1:23, 24). When it comes to knowing the way to heaven, there is no wisdom apart from the crucified Christ. When Paul says that in Christ 'are hidden all the treasures of wisdom and knowledge' (Colossians 2:3), he is referring to all those precious truths revealed to us by the Holy Spirit, which we would know nothing about if we were not the beneficiaries of his death. Christ is the wisdom of God because the plan of redemption is centred on him, both in its eternal origin and its execution.

All this is revealed to faith alone whereas human wisdom is acquired without faith, and is therefore not the kind of wisdom that embraces Christ. Indeed, the bankruptcy of the wisdom of those who are perishing is seen chiefly in the fact that it regards the message of the cross as foolishness (1 Corinthians 1:18). This is a sure test of the genuineness of our faith. If we regard the idea of being saved by a man called Jesus, put to death on a cross two thousand years ago as foolish, we may safely assume that we know nothing about divine wisdom. Since God's wisdom is revealed supremely in the message of the cross, those who reject the gospel remain blind to its wisdom. There is no ambiguity about Paul's teaching: 'For since in the wisdom of God the world through its wisdom did not know him, God was pleased through the foolishness of what was preached to save those who believe' (1 Corinthians 1:21). By using the word 'foolishness' in this verse, Paul is using the language of the natural man to whom the preaching of the Gospel does not make sense. How often do we find ourselves listening to religious debates on radio or television and being grieved by the blindness and folly of the intelligent and well-educated participants. We may listen to sermons in church with the same result! This is because the preacher himself is a stranger to the saving wisdom of God revealed in the person of Jesus Christ. 'The god of this age has blinded the minds of unbelievers, so that they cannot see the light of the gospel of the glory of Christ, who is the image of God' (2 Corinthians 4:4).

To digress for a moment – as with every aspect of gospel truth, we must be careful to distinguish between true faith and merely being 'religious.' Many people make much of the cross. They wear it round their necks and they cross themselves – we see footballers doing so as they enter and leave the field – but this, more often than not, is a substitute for the real thing. We need to remember that the Jews Paul speaks about were very religious, but they demanded miraculous signs before they would believe, signs that were not given. They expected a powerful Messiah who would deliver their nation from oppression and therefore, the idea of a crucified Messiah was ridiculous to them. They demanded miraculous signs before they would believe it (1 Corinthians 1:22).

In spite of Paul's teaching here, the late John Wimber introduced the notion of power evangelism, insisting that the preaching of the cross is largely ineffective unless accompanied by powerful signs. Many Christians accepted the idea. But Paul insists that the preaching of the gospel, although seen by the world as *powerless*, is in fact the *power* of God. We should never let go our belief that the preaching of the cross *alone* is effectual to the salvation of all for whom Christ died.

If then, we are to understand the cross and make good progress in the Christian life, we must always be aware of the danger of relying on our own wisdom. If we do not renounce our dependence on it we shall not grow in grace because as far as our eternal welfare is concerned, human wisdom is foolishness. Let us keep Paul's warning in mind: 'Do not deceive yourselves. If any one of you thinks he is wise by the standards of this age, he should become a *fool* so that he may become wise. For the wisdom of this world is foolishness in God's sight. As it is written: "He catches the wise in their craftiness," and again, "The Lord knows that the thoughts of the wise are futile"' (1 Corinthians 3:19, 20).

To come back to the point – the glory of the cross shines brightly to all who are endowed with the wisdom of God, and in comparison with that glory, all the passing glory of this age fades away.

4. The Believer's Boast

This brings us to another meaning of the word 'glory' (used as a verb) that was not mentioned in chapter one. To glory in something, means to boast or to exult in it. 'May I never boast except in the cross of our Lord Jesus Christ, through which the world has been crucified to me, and I to the world' (Galatians 6:14). The King James Version translates it: 'God forbid that I should glory, save in the cross of our Lord Jesus Christ...' The hymnwriter Isaac Watts (1674-1748) expresses it well:

> Forbid it, Lord, that I should boast,
> save in the cross of Christ my God:
> all the vain things that charm me most,
> I sacrifice them to his blood.

It may be difficult for us to think of boasting as anything other than verbal and pompous. Indeed, the meaning of 'boast' in the Oxford Reference Dictionary is 'to speak with great pride and try to impress people, to extol one's own excellence ...' But to boast in the cross has nothing to do with extolling one's own excellence. If we glory in the cross it is impossible to boast about ourselves. In addition, to glory in the cross is *much* more than words. It is a joyful exultation in our hearts because of what Jesus did for us on the cross. From the depth of our hearts we give God the glory for the cross!

Finally, to glory in the cross is never static. As we glory in our crucified Lord, more and more glory keeps on coming into view. The cross is where we *begin* to see ever-increasing glory in the Lord Jesus Christ – the glory of his resurrection, his exaltation, his glorious return, and the glory of that wonderful day when we shall see him as he is and be transformed into his likeness.

As long as the world remains, the glory of the crucified Christ will be the theme of the redeemed church and the joy of every member. Whatever else we may glory in will turn to dust. So 'let him who boasts boast in the Lord' (2 Corinthians 10:17). If we do not glory in Christ and him crucified, we are still strangers to his grace and blind to all spiritual truth.

CHAPTER FOUR

The Glory of His Exaltation

1. The Glory of His Humanity
2. The Glory of His Body
3. The Glory of His Lordship
4. The Glory of His High Priesthood
5. His Glory as Head of the Church

'Let us fix our eyes on Jesus, the author and Perfecter of our faith, who for the joy set before him endured the cross, scorning its shame, and sat down at the right hand of the throne of God' (Hebrews 12:2.)

The resurrection of Jesus Christ from the dead is the most important event in the history of the world. He is the only one who has conquered death and robbed it of its sting (1 Corinthians 15:55). He is the only one who has power to raise sinners from spiritual death and one day to raise them from physical death as well. In him alone resides the power to re-create all things so that they are free from every taint of sin. When Mary Magdalene and the other Mary went to the tomb at dawn and found it empty (Matthew 28:1-10), little did they realise that the wisdom and glory of God revealed in the resurrection of Jesus would one day fill the whole earth (Isaiah 11:9) and that both they and us would share in it. As the first sheaf of wheat was presented to the priest (Leviticus 23:10), so the resurrection of Jesus was the 'firstfruits of those who have fallen asleep' (1 Corinthians 15:20). And as the 'firstfruits' are the promise of an abundant harvest, so the resurrection of Christ is the 'firstfruit' of a spiritual harvest, the resurrection of all his redeemed people – all those who are predestined to share in his glory. According to John they are 'a great multitude that no one could count, from every nation, tribe, people and language' (Revelation 7:9). From a human point of view, that multitude is made up of all those who trust in

Jesus Christ for salvation: 'For my Father's will', said Jesus, 'is that everyone who looks to the Son and believes in him shall have eternal life, and I will raise him up at the last day' (John 6:40). Because Jesus lives, all who belong to that privileged throng may look forward to eternal life in the new heavens and new earth, the home of righteousness and peace.

It was for these reasons that the apostle Paul regarded the death, burial, and resurrection of Christ 'as of first importance' (1 Corinthians 15:3). The teaching and preaching of these earth-shaking events took precedence over everything else in his ministry. But this does not mean that Christ's exaltation and intercession are not also important. On the contrary, the salvation he purchased for us by his death and resurrection is secured by his exaltation and intercession, as we shall see in a moment.

1. The Glory of His Humanity

In common with many other soldiers, I was awarded medals for wartime service. Since it is not practical to wear the medals on the uniform except on ceremonial occasions, the ribbons only are worn in strips over the left breast pocket. Compared with other long-serving men, some of whom had so many honours it was difficult to cram them into the space available, I used to think my awards were rather paltry. I had room for many more!

We may be able to quantify honour in such cases but, as we saw in chapter one, when it comes to the glory of Christ it is impossible to do so. How can we speak of adding to or taking from the honour of him who in his eternal being was, and is, and always will be, infinitely and eternally glorious? 'For God was pleased to have all his fulness dwell in him...' (Colossians 1:19).

Even so, the Scriptures speak of further honours being conferred on him. And we, being human and finite creatures, cannot help wondering how glory can be added to the one who is already infinitely glorious. From our point of view, of course, there are new factors involved. The glory of Christ, which was not recognised in the Old Testament era, is now revealed so that we are privileged to see him for who he is – the eternal Son of God. As the apostle Peter explains, the Old Testament prophets 'searched intently and with the greatest care, trying to find out the time and circumstances to which the Spirit of Christ in them was pointing when he predicted the sufferings of Christ and the glories that would follow' (1 Peter 1:10, 11).

It would have been strange indeed if the Old Testament prophets, through whom the Spirit predicted these glories, were not themselves eager to know more about them. In the event however, it was revealed to them that the benefits of their ministry were intended, not for themselves, but for those who lived in the days when the prophecies reached their fulfilment (1 Peter 1:12). This means that it is we who live in the light of the New Testament revelation, who are the beneficiaries. Indeed, we have a double benefit. Not only do we profit from the further revelations of Christ's glory in the New Testament, but we also have a better understanding of the prophecies of the Old Testament – better even than the prophets themselves. We recognise that the teaching of the Old Testament on the matter of the glory of Christ (as on many other subjects) is for our benefit: 'For everything that was written in the past was written to teach us, so that through endurance and the encouragement of the Scriptures we might have hope' (Romans 15:4). How important it is then, that we make the most of our privileged position.

Sadly however, it is at this point that so many believers fail. Either we are unaware of what the prophets have spoken concerning the glory of Christ, or we pay little or no attention to it (Luke 24:25, 26). So many of us are not unlike the two dejected disciples who were walking to the village of Emmaus when the risen Christ caught up with them. These men were well aware of the Old Testament prophecies about the Messiah. More than that, they had been told by Jesus himself that 'the Son of Man must suffer many things and be rejected by the elders, chief priests and teachers of the law, and he must be killed and the third day be raised to life' (Luke 9:22). Yet, in spite of this, Jesus found it necessary to rebuke them: 'How foolish you are,' he said, 'and how slow of heart to believe all that the prophets have spoken! Did not Christ have to suffer these things and then enter his glory?' (Luke 24:25, 26). And it should be remembered that we have less excuse than these two disciples, because they did not have the benefit of the apostolic writings as we do.

Then, at his incarnation, he took our human nature. As a man he suffered and died; as a man he ascended to heaven; as a man he is seated 'at the right hand of God' (Hebrews 10:12) crowned with glory and honour, and as a man he will have dominion over all things. But we cannot doubt that from the divine standpoint, the glory of Christ conferred on him as our Redeemer, was his from eternity when the covenant of redemption was drawn up. The important thing, however, is the fact that our Saviour is infinitely glorious and occupies the place of highest honour in the church and in the universe.

Although we shall be like him when we see him, there are aspects of his glorified humanity that will not be true of ours. By his resurrection as a man, as well as *being* the eternal Son of God, he is now *declared* to be the Son of God. He is now the Son of God both in his divinity and his humanity. Speaking of his calling to preach the gospel, Paul explains that it is '...the gospel he promised beforehand through his prophets in the Holy Scriptures regarding his Son, who as to his human nature was a descendant of David, and who through the Spirit of holiness was declared with power to be the Son of God by his resurrection from the dead' (Romans 1:2-4). We too are sons of God, but our sonship is by grace and adoption into God's family. Christ's Sonship is his by right. As Calvin puts it: '...he possesses by nature what we acquire as a gift' (*Institutes,* Bk.2. para 6)

But we must guard against the idea that Jesus has become almighty in his manhood. He is still human (as well as divine), but his humanity is filled with the glory of the perfect graces and virtues of God himself. It is in this sense that we shall be like him – not in his divine power and glory, but in his perfect and glorious humanity. We are not destined to be equal with God.

The view we have by faith of his glory becomes even more captivating when we realise there is a man in heaven already glorified *for us*! Let us delve a little further into Hebrews 2:5-9, where we see our exalted Saviour honoured as our representative:

> "'What is man that you are mindful of him,
>   the son of man that you care for him?
> You made him a little lower than the angels;
>   you crowned him with glory and honour
>   and put everything under his feet.'"

In putting everything under him, God left nothing that is not subject to him. Yet at present we do not see everything subject to him. But we see Jesus, who was made a little lower than the angels, now crowned with glory and honour because he suffered death, so that by the grace of God he might taste death for everyone.'

The quotation at the beginning of the text is from Psalm 8:3-6 where the psalmist, after considering the glory of the heavens, the moon and the stars which God has set in place, expresses his wonder that God should care for man: 'What is man that you are mindful of him, the son of man that you care for him?' The evidence of God's care for man is that he made him a little (or for a little while) lower than the angels, crowned him with glory and honour and put everything under his feet. The psalmist almost certainly had Genesis 1:26 in mind which speaks of God giving man authority over the earth and all its creatures. But as we saw in the last chapter, this great honour has not yet been realised. Man has failed to achieve it. But the wonderful news is that in the exaltation of Christ, God's purpose is already accomplished. Although we do not yet see man in that position of supreme honour, we do see the man Jesus *crowned with glory and honour*. As our representative he too was made for a little while lower than the angels in order to accomplish our complete redemption, and now he is seated at the right hand of the Majesty in heaven (Hebrews 8:1). Our exaltation as the crown of creation is therefore secured.

2. The Glory of His Body

The Greek philosophers tended to regard the human body as vile, and only the soul imprisoned within it as good. This opened the way for the bizarre notion that the soul is not affected by the sins of the body, so that we can sin as much as we like without defiling the soul! In this scheme of things, redemption is seen as the re-uniting of the soul with its Maker after being delivered from its vile bodily prison.

We find no support for such a view in the Bible, except that in some respects the human body is indeed portrayed as vile. Our mortality, bringing with it all our physical suffering, is the result of sin's curse (Romans 5:12). Humus we are, and to humus we shall return (Genesis 3:19). 'Our bodies were made vile by the entrance of sin' says John Owen, the great Bible scholar of the Puritan era, 'thence they become brothers to the worms, and sisters unto corruption' (John Owen, *Works,* Volume 1).

I cannot help associating the vileness of the body with the stench of death – a stench I first encountered during the rapid advance of Allied armies through Northern France in 1944. I came across it again when I entered the Belsen concentration camp shortly after its liberation. Just once or twice since then I have detected it when conducting a service of interment at the graveside in intense heat. After one such occasion, the undertaker apologised to me: 'Sorry about the smell' he said! I suspect the coffin lid was not fastened down properly. We do all we can, of course, to conceal the offensiveness of it. A dead body in the hands of an embalmer can be made to look radiantly healthy. Without his skills, to have the body of the deceased on show, as is still the custom in many places, would be far too distressing for the mourners. The corruption cannot be hidden for long.

Against this dismal and depressing background, Paul's words are a ray of light that transforms our entire outlook as far as our human bodies are concerned: 'But our citizenship is in heaven' he says, 'And we eagerly await a Saviour from there, the Lord Jesus Christ, who, by the power that enables him to bring everything under his control, will transform our lowly bodies so that they will be like his glorious body' (Philippians 3:20, 21).

The resurrection is proof that the body Jesus took from the womb of the virgin Mary has not been given up, but glorified. The New Testament provides several clues as to what the resurrection body of Christ was like, so that we have at least a little idea what ours will be like. We know that he passed through closed doors into the presence of the disciples. They thought they were seeing a ghost, but Jesus said to them: 'Look at my hands and my feet. It is I myself! Touch me and see; a ghost does not have flesh and bones, as you see I have' (Luke 24:39; John 20:19). And as glorious as his resurrection body must have been, his glorified body must be still more glorious. We have a limited insight into the nature of it from the account of the events on 'a high mountain' where 'he was transfigured before them. His face shone like the sun, and his clothes became as white as light' (Matthew 17:2). The event reminds us of Paul's description of God as living 'in unapproachable light' (1 Timothy 6:16) and also of the Psalmist's portrayal of God wrapping 'himself in light as with a garment' (Psalm 104:2). But apart from these glimpses, a veil has been drawn over the nature of Christ's glorious body. We would not be able to cope with more than is revealed anyway.

3. The Glory of His Lordship

The apostle John describes a vision he had in these words: 'I saw heaven standing open and there before me was a white horse, whose rider is called Faithful and True... His eyes are like blazing fire, and on his head are many crowns... He is dressed in a robe dipped in blood, and his name is the Word of God ... Out of his mouth comes a sharp sword with which to strike down the nations... On his robe and on his thigh he has this name written: KING OF KINGS AND LORD OF LORDS' (Revelation 19:11-16).

What glory is revealed in these symbols! Our Lord Jesus is the one who is Faithful and True, from whose eyes nothing is hidden. He is the one who is victorious over all his enemies. He is the one who will subdue them with the sharp two-edged sword of the word of God (See Revelation 1:16 and Hebrews 4:12). The many crowns speak of his dominion over all, for he is not just a king among kings, but a King over all kings.

The Old Testament prophecies of his kingship are also unmistakable. Take Jeremiah 23:5 for example: '"The days are coming," declares the LORD, "when I will raise up to David a righteous Branch, a King who will reign wisely and do what is just and right in the land."' The prophet is affirming that the Lord will keep his promise of a King of David's dynasty to reign forever over God's people (2 Samuel 7:16). Just as a branch shoots from the stump of a felled tree, so the King of kings will arise from the fallen dynasty of King David of Israel. The stump represents the godly remnant of the church in the Old Testament, the Israel of God. This is in keeping with several Old Testament prophecies. The prophet Isaiah speaks of the kingship of Christ in this way: 'Of the increase of his government and peace there will be no end. He will reign on David's throne and over his kingdom, establishing and upholding it with righteousness and justice from that time on and for ever' (Isaiah 9:7). And again in Isaiah 11:1 'A shoot will come up from the stump of Jesse; from his roots a Branch will bear fruit' (Jesse was the father of David).

Jesus himself was fully aware of his honoured position. We read that during his triumphal entry into Jerusalem, the Pharisees protested because the disciples began joyfully to praise God in loud voices: 'Blessed is the king who comes in the name of the Lord.' But Jesus dismissed their protest: "'I tell you" he replied, "if they keep quiet, the stones will cry out…"' (Luke 19:37-40). When Pilate asked Jesus if he were a king, he did not deny it (John 18:37). And he said to his disciples: 'All authority in heaven and on earth has been given to me...' (Matthew 28:18). He had previously said to them that 'The Father loves the Son and has placed everything in his hands' (John 3:35).

When we turn to the letters of Paul, yet more glory shines. The power of God in the conversion of sinners, says the apostle, 'is like the working of his mighty strength, which he exerted in Christ when he raised him from the dead and seated him at his right hand in the heavenly realms, far above all rule and authority, power and dominion, and every title that can be given, not only in the present age but also in the one to come' (Ephesians 1:19-21). There can be little doubt that these words express the apostle's conviction that Christ's exaltation is the fulfilment of Psalm 110:1, where David says: 'The LORD says to my Lord: "Sit at my right hand until I make your enemies a footstool for your feet."' David, the king of Israel here speaks of another man who is the king's 'Lord', a man who is waiting until all his enemies surrender to his supreme authority, and that man is Jesus.

In Paul's letter to the Philippians, we have a sublime description of the honour bestowed on Jesus, and revealed to us as a reward for his accomplishment:

> Therefore God exalted him to the highest place
> and gave him the name that is above every name,
> that at the name of Jesus every knee should bow,
> in heaven and on earth and under the earth,
> and every tongue confess that Jesus Christ is Lord,
> to the glory of God the Father.
>
> *(Philippians 2:9-11).*

The word 'therefore' at the beginning of this quotation is important. As an example for his readers to follow, the apostle has just been describing the attitude of Christ in his astonishing condescension and humiliation – he who was God did not count equality with God something to be grasped, but humbled himself and became obedient to death. And then he tells them what God thought about his Son. The great honour bestowed on him was a direct consequence of his obedience and humiliation. It was, in other words, a reward.

But what is the name above every name? Many believers assume it is simply the name 'Jesus' now invested with greater honour, but there is much more to it than this. To the apostle, a Jew, there was only one name that is above every name. It was the name 'Jehovah.' In the Old Testament 'Jehovah' (Yahweh) is the name for God (translated 'Lord' in the New International Version.) Paul is saying that 'Jesus is Jehovah,' and that to confess him as such is to glorify God the Father.

We must be careful however to guard against the idea that Jesus *became* Lord as a reward for his obedience. The Scriptures leave us in no doubt that his divine glory is eternal. For example, the apostle John tells us that when Isaiah 'saw the Lord' (Isaiah 6:1), what he saw was the glory of Jesus! (John 12:41). Jesus was, is, and always will be Jehovah. We are familiar with Isaiah's graphic description of the suffering of the Lord's servant (Isaiah 53), and as believers we do not hesitate to identify the servant as Jesus, but we tend to overlook the fact that the glory of Jesus and Jehovah is one and the same. The prophet saw the seraphs and heard them '…calling to one another: "Holy, holy, holy is the Lord Almighty; the whole earth is full of his glory"' (Isaiah 6:3). And what was the prophet's reaction? '"Woe to me"' he cried. '"I am ruined! For I am a man of unclean lips, and I live among a people of unclean lips, and my eyes have seen the King, the Lord Almighty"' (Isaiah 6:5). Isaiah then, leaves us in no doubt that what he saw was the glory of Jehovah, and John makes it absolutely clear that what Isaiah saw was the glory of Jesus!

Isaiah also tells us that the child born to us – the child born in Bethlehem centuries later – 'will be called Wonderful Counsellor, Mighty God, Everlasting Father, Prince of Peace' whose government will never end (Isaiah 9:6). How can such titles be given to anyone other than Jehovah? Some time ago a member of the so-called 'Jehovah's Witnesses' called at my door and tried to convince me that Jesus could not be equal with Jehovah because Isaiah says his name is 'Mighty God' and not 'Almighty God.' She had obviously not been briefed about the words that follow and was nonplussed when I pointed them out to her.

As with his glory, so also with his power. He has power to ensure the safety of his people and to subdue all their enemies. 'He will stand and shepherd his flock in the strength of the LORD, in the majesty of the LORD his God; And they will live securely, for then his greatness will reach to the end of the earth. And he will be their peace' (Micah 5:4, 5). His power over his enemies will be seen when he brings destruction on all who do not obey him, and casts the beast and the false prophet into the lake of fire (Revelation 19:20).

In his vision recorded in Revelation chapters four and five, the apostle John sees a throne in heaven with someone sitting on it (4:2). Without doubt it is the Lord Jesus Christ (see Acts 7:54-56). His glory is described in symbolic terms as having the appearance of jasper and carnelian, and a rainbow resembling an emerald, encircles the throne. Surrounding the throne were twenty-four other thrones on which were seated twenty-four elders dressed in white with gold crowns on their heads. These represent the redeemed church now perfected in holiness. Flashes of lightning and peals of thunder come from the throne and seven blazing lamps, symbolising the Holy Spirit in all his perfection. Four living creatures round the throne – perhaps representing the angels – never stop saying: ... 'Holy, holy, holy is the Lord God Almighty, who was, and is, and is to come' (4:8).

Then John sees a scroll in the hand of him who sat on the throne, sealed with seven seals. And a mighty angel asks, 'Who is worthy to break the seals and open the scroll?' (5:2). Most serious Bible scholars agree that the opening of the scroll represents the unveiling of God's eternal purpose that will explain the meaning of the world's history. Only the Lord Jesus Christ is worthy to open the seals.

Finally, '…the voice of many angels, numbering thousands upon thousands, and ten thousand times ten thousand' (5:11), sing praises to the Lamb: 'Worthy is the Lamb, who was slain, to receive power and wealth and wisdom and strength and honour and glory and praise' (5:12). 'To him who sits on the throne and to the Lamb be praise and honour and glory and power, for ever and ever!' (5:13).

We must be careful not to take the details of the vision too literally. The important point is that God is on the throne of the universe, and Christ alone is qualified to reveal the eternal counsels of God because he was slain and with his blood purchased men for God from every tribe and language and people and nation (5:9). No one else can explain the meaning and purpose of life – only the Lion of the tribe of Judah, the Lamb of God (5:5, 6).

What then do we affirm about the Lord Jesus? We believe there is no other name – be it the name of a monarch, lord, emperor, dictator or ruler, in this world or the world to come, greater than the name of Christ. He is Lord of lords and King of kings.

4. The Glory of His High Priesthood

If we asked for an audience with the Queen we would, to say the least, encounter a number of difficulties. Almost certainly we would be refused, or perhaps fobbed off with an interview with a palace official. We simply do not have the right just to walk into the Queen's presence and speak with her. If this is the case with an earthly monarch, what chance do we stand of having an audience with God himself? How can sinners have the right to come into his holy presence? Yet, wonder of wonders, we who belong to Christ have access into his presence at any time. And at the end of our days on this earth, we shall be admitted to his glorious presence forever. How and why was this astonishing privilege conferred upon us?

The question 'Why?' has no answer. Why God should love us as he does, and not others, is a mystery. But to answer the question 'How?' we need to go back into the Old Testament. Before Christ came into the world, the temple in Jerusalem (and the tent in the desert that preceded it) was the place where God's glory was revealed (1 Kings 8:10, 11). The inner sanctuary, in which the ark of the covenant was placed and over which stood two cherubim carved in olive wood (1 Kings 6:23), was the most holy place in the temple. It was separated from the rest of the temple by a veil. It was out of bounds to everyone except the high priest, and he was permitted to enter but once a year on the Day of Atonement (Leviticus 16:32-34). The high priest acting as a mediator between God and his chosen people, offered sacrifices for their sins, as well as for his own.

This ritual was temporary, but very significant. It pointed forward to the sacrifice of Christ and his entrance into the presence of God on our behalf. That is to say, the function of the high priest in going through the veil into the most holy place is a pattern of the priestly work of Christ. The writer to the Hebrews explains: 'But only the high priest entered the inner room, and that only once a year, and never without blood, which he offered for himself and for the sins the people had committed in ignorance. The Holy Spirit was showing by this that the way into the Most Holy Place had not yet been disclosed as long as the first tabernacle was still standing...' But when Christ came as high priest, 'he went through the greater and more perfect tabernacle that is not man-made, that is to say, not a part of this creation. He did not enter by means of the blood of goats and calves; but he entered the Most Holy Place once for all by his own blood, having obtained eternal redemption' (Hebrews 9:7, 8, 11, 12).

We see then, that the privilege of entering without fear into the presence of God was obtained for us by our great high priest, the Lord Jesus Christ. He is both priest and victim. He entered the presence of God with his own blood, which means that his intercession on our behalf as priest is based on his sacrifice at the cross as victim

– a sacrifice that is sufficient for the sins of the world and therefore need not be repeated. This is in sharp contrast with the sacrifices made by the priests of the Old Testament which could never take away sins. 'But when this priest' (the Lord Jesus) 'had offered for all time one sacrifice for sins, he sat down at the right hand of God... because by one sacrifice he has made perfect for ever those who are being made holy' (Hebrews 10:12-14).

Back in the nineteen-seventies when I was minister of a church in St Helens, Merseyside, a bitter industrial dispute crippled the Pilkington Glass Works for thirteen weeks. Relationships between the two sides had completely broken down. The management was not prepared to trust the men to conduct their own ballot because there had been some shady dealing. But neither were the men prepared to accept the dictates of the management. Someone had to be found who would represent the management to the men and the men to the management; someone who was just and fair, and understood the grievances of the workmen. In the end the clergy of the town were asked if they would do it, and we found ourselves in the middle of a very hostile situation. Eventually, when the ballot we supervised resulted in a vote to return to work, some of the men were still not satisfied and accused us of rigging the ballot. But happily they were overruled, and the strike was over. We were certainly acting as mediators, but we had no power to make peace.

The role of Jesus as our Mediator is very different. As our 'go-between' he *does* have the power to make peace. He does not act as an arbitrator without power. He not only paid the price for our sin, without which reconciliation would not have been possible, but he also ensures that his death will not be in vain in the case of all for whom he died. He has the power to establish reconciliation between God and his people and will not fail to do so. He does not put pressure on them or violate their wills, but lovingly persuades them that it is in their best interests to be at peace with God. If we see no glory in this, I think we may safely conclude we know nothing about being reconciled to God.

His glory as our Mediator continues forever. When the apostle John says: 'But if anybody does sin, we have one who speaks to the Father in our defence – Jesus Christ, the Righteous One' (1 John 2:1), he is not thinking of Jesus speaking to the Father just once and no more, but as continuing this ministry as long as this world lasts. According to the writer to the Hebrews, this is one of the important differences between our High Priest and the Old Testament priests: 'Now there were many of those priests, since death prevented them from continuing in office; but because Jesus lives for ever, he has a permanent priesthood. Therefore he is able to save completely those who come to God through him, because he always lives to intercede for them' (Hebrews 7:25).

The honour of being high priest in the Old Testament was not something that anyone could take upon himself. He had to be called by God, as the writer to the Hebrews explains: 'No one takes this honour upon himself; he must be called by God, just as Aaron was.' This was also true of the Lord Jesus: 'So Christ also did not take upon himself the glory of becoming a high priest. But God said to him, "You are my Son; today I have become your Father"' (Hebrews 5:4, 5). Christ's fitness for the office of High Priest for-ever stems from the fact that he was the Father's Son. No one else was fit to take up the office.

The writer goes on to say of Christ: 'You are a priest for ever in the order of Melchizedek' (7:17). Now Melchizedek is a mysterious figure. He is the 'king of Salem' who blessed Abraham (Genesis 14:18-20), and to whom David refers in Psalm 110:4. Some think he was a pre-incarnation appearance of Christ, but whoever he was, the point is that Melchizedek was 'without beginning of days or end of life' and was clearly superior to Abraham (Hebrews 7:3, 4). Christ's priesthood is of the same order, and it is therefore a priest-hood without end. Together with the first verse of the same Psalm to which I referred earlier, and of course with the benefit of New Testament teaching, we have in Psalm 110 a remarkable display of the glory of Christ as both Priest and King.

5. His Glory as Head of the Church

'Why does the Lord bother with the church?' The question is usually posed by believers who have grown weary of petty squabbling, false teaching, superficial innovations and the like. These things are regrettable to us, and no doubt grievous to him. But we need to remember that 'Christ loved the church and gave himself up for her to make her holy...' (Ephesians 5:25, 26), and no matter how imperfect she is, he will never forsake her. If this were not true, the church would have disappeared long ago. This is not a recipe for complacency, however; we all have a solemn duty to promote holiness and harmony in the church, and we do not take it as seriously as we ought.

Before we go further, we must be clear what Paul means by 'church.' He is not thinking of an organisation or a building. He is not even thinking only of a local gathering of believers. His address to his first letter to the Corinthians tells us what he has in mind: 'To the church of God in Corinth, to those sanctified in Christ Jesus and called to be holy, together with all those everywhere who call in the name of Lord Jesus Christ – their Lord and ours' (1 Corinthians 1:2). Indeed, these words would serve as a definition of the church. Of course, Paul does use the word 'church' to describe a local assembly of believers – the church in Corinth, Antioch, Jerusalem or wherever – but he sees the local church as an integral part of the universal church, made up of all those whose names are written in the Lamb's book of life (Revelation 21:27). Nothing can prevail against the true church of Christ (Matthew 16:18), but church organisations, denominations, and church buildings are expendable.

My home is near the sea, and the other evening as the sun was setting, I looked across the bay. The visibility was poor and the distant shoreline was fading from view. But the sun was being reflected with astonishing brightness from what could only be windows of some kind. Of all the panes of glass in the buildings on the far side, just two or three were reflecting the light.

How like the church in our land today, I thought! Just one here and another there faithfully holding forth the word of life and reflecting the glory of Jesus, while the remainder blend with the twilight. But as I mused, my mind turned to the glory of that day soon coming, when Jesus will return and everything that now prevents the church radiating his glory will be removed for ever. On that day, we who belong to him will reflect his glory as never before, for we shall be completely changed by the sight of him. And not only that, we shall admire his beauty in a manner never before possible. He who is now admired by angels will be glorified in his people and be glorified by them. Jesus is coming again says Paul, 'to be glorified in his holy people and to be marvelled at among all those who have believed' (2 Thessalonians 1:10). The glory of that day will greatly exceed our wildest dreams.

Speaking of angels reminds me of another Pauline theme in Ephesians 3:8-11: 'Although I am less than the least of all God's people, this grace was given me: to preach to the Gentiles the unsearchable riches in Christ, and to make plain to everyone the administration of this mystery, which for ages past was kept hidden in God, who created all things. His intent was that now, through the church, the manifold wisdom of God should be made known to the rulers and authorities in the heavenly realms, according to his eternal purpose which he accomplished in Christ Jesus our Lord.' At first sight the passage seems rather daunting, but, as with many apparently difficult passages, it will yield precious truths to the patient student – truths that should warm the heart of every Christian. The apostle speaks first of his high calling to preach to the Gentiles 'the unsearchable riches in Christ' – to make known to them the wealth of glories to be found in him. But at this point, Paul's horizon broadens as he goes on to speak of his vocation 'to make plain to everyone the administration of this mystery' which formerly God had kept hidden. What does he mean?

The mystery now being revealed is not, as some think, merely the admission of the Gentiles into the church, but the mystery of

God's eternal plan of redemption itself (see Romans 16:25); the reconciliation between Jew and Gentile being the fruit of it. The gospel is not an emergency plan to meet an unexpected situation, but the timely unfolding of God's eternal plan. But what did God intend by the revelation of this mystery?

This answer to this question is surprising, and should never be forgotten. God intends that the 'manifold wisdom of God' revealed in his plan of redemption – his love and justice in choosing and saving sinners, making them holy, and bringing them without fail to glory – should be exhibited *in the church*. But what is even more surprising, even breathtaking, is the fact that the observers are the angels in heaven and not, in this case, the people in the world.

What an astonishing truth this is! It is God's purpose that angels, here described as 'rulers and authorities in the heavenly realms,' should learn about the glory of Christ in the gospel from the church! In a sense, the church has a similar function to creation. Just as creation manifests the glory of God's eternal power and deity to men (Romans 1:20), so the church reveals the glories of God's plan of redemption to angels. The final consummation of the church – her completion and perfection – will of course be the most glorious exhibition of the glory of our redemption in Christ, but that glory must also be visible in the meantime.

This being so, some serious questions arise, the most obvious being – what are the angels learning about the manifold wisdom of God in our redemption, by what they observe in the church to which we belong? Do they see Christ being uplifted in our worship, and honoured in our fellowship? Or is his glory being obscured by our petty-mindedness, self-righteousness, self-interest, and childish bickering? In other words, do the angels see a Christ-centred or a self-centred church? It might well make a big difference in the life of the church if every believer became deeply aware of our angelic spectators, although since we already know that the Lord's eyes are upon us, one wonders.

Finally, the biblical principle that the Lord Jesus Christ is to be the focus of the church's worship, is clear from Paul's doxology: 'Now to him who is able to do immeasurably more than all we ask or imagine, according to his power that is at work within us, to him be glory in the church and in Christ Jesus throughout all generations for ever and ever! Amen' (Ephesians 3:20, 21). The church as a whole, and every single member, has a duty to give glory to God through the Lord Jesus Christ, and to glorify him in everything we say and do. When the glory of Christ becomes the overriding concern of the church, whatever spoils our worship, witness, and fellowship, will not be tolerated. Our individual contribution will be seen in a new light. Why? Because those who have a settled will and an enduring desire to glorify our exalted Lord will not stand on their pride, harbour grievances or pursue vendettas. Nor will they come to terms with those who want to dilute the gospel and compromise on Christian morality. They will keep their eyes fixed on Jesus.

CHAPTER FIVE

The Role of the Holy Spirit

1. He Reveals Christ's Glory to us
2. He reveals Christ's Glory through us
3. He Baptises us into One Body

'But when he, the Spirit of truth, comes, he will guide you into all truth. He will not speak on his own; he will speak only what he hears... He will bring glory to me by taking from what is mine and making it known to you.
John 16:13, 14.

1. He Reveals Christ's Glory to us

High up in the roof of the darkened theatre a man is operating a spotlight. His task is to keep the ballet dancer on the stage far below, in the centre of the circle of light. Where the dancer goes, the light goes. Such is the skill of the operator, the people in the audience are hardly aware of his presence Their eyes are fixed on the dancer.

To keep the spotlight on Jesus is the task of the Holy Spirit, and this he delights to do. Whenever and wherever the glory of Jesus is revealed, the Spirit of God is at work, even though those to whom it is revealed may not be aware of it. There is no inconsistency here with what is said elsewhere about Jesus himself being the one who reveals the Father to us. In Matthew 11:27 for example, Jesus says: 'All things have been committed to me by my Father. No one knows the Father except the Son and those to whom the Son chooses to reveal him.' Although in the plan of redemption the Spirit has the particular task of revealing the glory of Christ, there is perfect unity of purpose between the persons of the Trinity, both the Son and the Spirit being pleased to do the Father's will. What are the implications? The Spirit does not act independently of the Father and the Son; he is not at the beck and call of anybody, but is sovereign in all he does. (So let us stop trying to tell him when to come and when to go.)

The teaching of Jesus on the role of the Spirit is clear: 'He will bring glory to me by taking from what is mine and making it known to you. All that belongs to the Father is mine. That is why I said the Spirit will take from what is mine and make it known to you' (John 16:14-15). Just as the Son was sent to reveal the glory of the Father (John 1:18), so the Holy Spirit is sent to reveal the glory of the Son, and in this the Father is glorified. And just as the Son brings glory to the Father, so the Spirit brings glory to the Son. This is the pinnacle of the Spirit's achievement. He does not seek to improve on the glory of Jesus by adding further glory of his own as many seem to think. The idea is deeply offensive, not only to the Lord Jesus Christ, but also to the Spirit himself.

The Holy Spirit is called 'the Spirit of truth' because he reveals Jesus, and Jesus is the truth. The truth cannot be separated from his person. Jesus is the embodiment of truth in the sense that he is the source of truth about the Father. When Jesus referred to himself as being 'the truth' we cannot doubt that this is what he meant (John 14:6). The Spirit also reveals the moral excellence of Jesus's character so that we have an example to live by. This, as the context shows, is what Paul had in mind when he spoke of the 'truth that is in Jesus' (Ephesians 4:21) Jesus was a faithful witness to the truth during his ministry on earth, and in his absence the Spirit carries on the same work. Further confirmation is to be found in John 15:26 where Jesus makes clear that 'the Spirit of truth' is so-called because he will reveal the truth about Jesus: 'When the Counsellor comes, whom I will send from the Father, the Spirit of truth who goes out from the Father, he will testify about me...'

Since the final revelation of truth in Jesus (as distinct from the partial revelations in the Old Testament) is now contained within the pages of the Bible, the Spirit's task is to open our minds to the

Scriptures. He guided the writers of God's word so that the truth may be preserved for us (2 Peter 1:21), and now he applies the truth of the inspired word to the hearts of those whom he chooses, convicting them of sin and showing them their need of a Saviour (1 Thessalonians 1:5). But his work does not stop there; by the same means he reveals Jesus to us day by day so that we may grow in his likeness. Paul expresses it like this: 'God chose you to be saved through the sanctifying work of the Spirit and through belief in the truth' (2 Thessalonians 2:13). We must always take great care not to separate the Spirit's work from God's word.

Nor must we separate the gift of the Spirit from the blessing of redemption. According to the apostle to the Gentiles, Christ redeemed us from the curse *in order that* 'the blessing given to Abraham might come to the Gentiles through Christ Jesus, so that by faith we might receive the promise of the Spirit' (Galatians 3:13, 14). For that promise to be fulfilled in our lives it is necessary only to be redeemed from the curse (Genesis 3:17-19). This being the case, the idea that we must seek the gift of the Spirit by faith *after* we are redeemed is completely ruled out. It is the Spirit who does the seeking according to his sovereign will; if this were not true, we would not be redeemed. The idea of being redeemed without the Spirit is too absurd for words.

Paul's teaching in Romans 8:9, 10 is particularly instructive. 'You, however, are not controlled by the sinful nature but by *the Spirit*, if *the Spirit of God* lives in you. And if anyone does not have *the Spirit of Christ*, he does not belong to *Christ.*' Notice the four titles in (my) italics in these verses. First, the apostle refers to 'the Spirit,' then 'the Spirit of God', then 'the Spirit of Christ,' and then just 'Christ.' All these terms are interchangeable. The Spirit, the Spirit of God, and the Spirit of Christ, are titles of the Holy Spirit. Paul's meaning could not be clearer. If Christ is in us, then so is the Holy Spirit, and if the Holy Spirit is in us, so is Christ. People who are not born of the Spirit through faith in Christ are not Christians, and any teaching on the Holy Spirit that even so much as hints that the Spirit gives blessings that are separate from or superior to the blessings we have received in Christ, is bogus.

The gift of the Spirit is described in Scripture as an anointing. In the Old Testament people were anointed with oil to signify their special relationship with God (2 Samuel 2:4), and anointing was associated with the gift of the Spirit, as in Isaiah 61:1: 'The Spirit of the Sovereign LORD is on me, because the LORD has anointed me to preach good news to the poor'. Jesus said that these words were fulfilled in himself (Luke 4:18-21). Peter too, in his sermon to Cornelius and his household, referred to Jesus as the one whom God anointed with the Holy Spirit (Acts 10:38). Material things separated for holy use were also anointed (Exodus 30:22-29). Although carried out by men, anointing was regarded as an act of God (1 Samuel 10:1) and was therefore held in high esteem.

It is with this symbolism in mind that the outpouring of the Spirit on believers in the New Testament is seen as an anointing. The Lord Jesus was, of course, anointed for a very special task, but this must not blind us to the fact that *every* believer is seen as being anointed with the Holy Spirit, and by this means we too are set apart for God's service. 'Now it is God' says Paul, 'who makes us and you stand firm in Christ. He anointed us, set his seal of ownership on us, and put his Spirit into our hearts as a deposit, guaranteeing what is to come' (2 Corinthians 1:21, 22). It is patently obvious that the apostle is not restricting the anointing to those who are called to some special ministry but to all Christians without exception. John confirms this: 'But you have an anointing from the Holy One, and all of you know the truth,'... 'As for you, the anointing you have received from him remains in you, and you do not need anyone to teach you. But as his anointing teaches you about all things and as that anointing is real, not counterfeit – just as it has taught you, remain in him' (1 John 2:20, 27).

By the term 'the Holy One' John is almost certainly referring to the Lord Jesus Christ (See Mark 1:24; John 6:69; Acts 3:14). He is the one who anoints all God's children with the Holy Spirit, an anointing that *remains* in them. The Spirit is competent to teach them all they need to know about Christ, even if they have no teacher, and all they need to know is contained within the pages of Holy Scripture. The anointing of the Spirit then is God's seal of ownership and the means whereby all the precious truths about Christ and our salvation through him, are revealed to us so that we are equipped for his service. (John is not telling his readers that teachers are now no longer needed; otherwise he would not be teaching them himself. The point John is making is this: teachers cannot teach without the Spirit, but the Spirit *can* teach without teachers).

What hope would there be for the church without the teaching ministry of the Spirit? And since God's church is holy by virtue of being indwelt by the Spirit, how careful we ought to be that we teach what the Spirit teaches; in other words, that our teaching is biblical. To do otherwise is a recipe for insecurity and instability. Paul found it necessary to warn the church in Corinth about this very thing. With false teachers in mind – teachers who added to the apostolic revelation – he said: 'Don't you know that you yourselves are God's temple, and that God's Spirit lives in you? If anyone destroys God's temple, God will destroy him: for God's temple is sacred, and you are that temple' (1 Corinthians 3:16, 17). There is an Old Testament precedent for Paul's stance here. The penalty for defiling the temple under Old Testament law was death or excommunication (Leviticus 15:31; Numbers 19:20). False teaching is an offence against the Spirit and defiles the church. It should therefore be treated with much more seriousness than it is at present.

Further light is shed on the role of the Spirit in John 16:8-11 where Jesus says: 'When he' (the Spirit) 'comes, he will convict the world of guilt in regard to sin and righteousness and judgement: in regard to sin, because men do not believe in me; in regard to righteousness, because I am going to the Father...and in regard to judgement, because the prince of this world now stands condemned.' Notice how all three aspects of the Spirit's work focus on but one subject – the Lord Jesus Christ. Why does the Spirit convince people in regard to sin? Because there is no greater sin than rejecting Christ. Why does the Spirit convince people in regard to righteousness? Because the proof of Christ's perfect righteousness against all the charges to the contrary, is seen in his resurrection and ascension to the Father. And why does the Spirit convince people in regard to judgement? Because in the death of Christ, the judgement of Satan has already taken place and all who reject Christ are under the same judgement.

If we are looking for evidences of being taught by the Spirit, high on the list alongside an eagerness to glorify Christ, will be the depth of our gratitude to God, gratitude that is usually expressed in Trinitarian terms. We shall find ourselves thanking the Father that the Spirit has revealed and applied the benefits of Christ's sacrifice to our hearts. The apostles frequently speak of our redemption in this Trinitarian manner. Peter tells us that 'we have been chosen according to the foreknowledge of God the Father, through the sanctifying work of the Spirit, for obedience to Jesus Christ...' (1 Peter 1:2). Paul tells the Ephesian believers that he keeps 'asking that the God of our Lord Jesus Christ, the glorious Father, may give you the Spirit of wisdom and revelation, so that you may know him better (Ephesians 1:17). He also prays that out of the Father's glorious riches 'he may strengthen you with power through his Spirit in your inner being, so that Christ may dwell in your hearts through faith' (Ephesians 3:16, 17). The perfect harmony between the three Persons of the Trinity prohibits indebtedness to one Person more than another. In 2 Corinthians 3:17, 18, Paul shows that it is impossible that there should be any disparity between the work of the Son and that of the Spirit: 'Now the Lord is the Spirit, and where the Spirit of the Lord is, there is freedom. And we, who with unveiled faces all reflect the Lord's glory, are being transformed into his likeness with ever-increasing glory, which comes from the Lord, who is the Spirit.' Throughout the New Testament, the word 'Lord' means the Lord Jesus. Paul is therefore saying that Christ and the Holy Spirit are one, and are in perfect harmony with each other.

Sadly, the prominence given in the New Testament to the glory of Christ as the main focus of the Spirit's ministry is not reflected in the teaching or the practice of many, if not most churches in our land today. Nor does it find much expression in our prayers. Instead of echoing requests like those expressed in Paul's prayer for the Ephesian believers, that we may be enlightened by the Spirit in order that we may know 'the hope to which he has called us, the riches of his glorious inheritance in the saints' (Ephesians 1:18), we pray for (what we think are) uplifting spiritual experiences for their own sake – experiences that bear little or no relation to the teaching of Scripture and teach us nothing about our hope or the riches of our inheritance. In the long term, this is bound to leave us dissatisfied and insecure. (The parallel with the drug culture is too disturbing to ignore). Should we not rather be praising God for his wonderful redemption? Should we not be asking him to open our minds and hearts more and more to the glory of Christ in which we shall share one day? 'No eye has seen,' says Paul, 'no ear has heard, no mind has conceived what God has prepared for those who love him – but God has revealed it to us by his Spirit' (1 Corinthians 2:9, 10).

Although these revelations were made to the apostles by the Spirit, they are also revealed to us by the same Spirit through their writings. Why then should we be hankering after subjective and indefinite experiences when the glory of our future destiny is there to be unearthed? May God bring us to that place where our hearts are overflowing with gratitude because he is pleased to reveal to us what cannot be discovered by human reason. Such gratitude will never fade, but will always be growing deeper, for the simple reason that the Spirit does not reveal truth as a conjuror reveals a rabbit from a hat and then causes it to disappear again. The Spirit reveals truth by actually conveying grace to us so that we are able to understand it and assimilate it. This is how we grow in confidence that we really are the beneficiaries of the saving work of Christ. When it comes to spiritual blessings, there is none greater.

In summary, with the Spirit within and the Scriptures to hand, we have all the treasures of wisdom and knowledge available to us (Colossians 2:3), and as we make progress in the Christian life, the Spirit will reveal more and more of these endless treasures that are all ours in Christ. We have inherited a gold mine that contains limitless wealth, and since the Spirit is the one who knows his way around, he is the one to show us where all the gold is!

To those who see no glory in Jesus – no matter what other 'spiritual' experiences they may have had – we affirm that they know nothing of the work of the Spirit and therefore nothing of the blessings of the Christian life. They are still under condemnation (John 3:18).

2. He reveals Christ's Glory through us

As believers we need to be constantly reminding ourselves that we are 'the light of the world' (Matthew 5:14). We are rubbing shoulders with people every day who are walking in darkness; they do not know why they are here or where they are going. People do not light a lamp, Jesus said, and put in under a bowl but on its stand, so that it gives light to everyone in the house. 'In the same way' he continued, 'let your light shine before men, that they may see you good deeds and praise your Father in heaven' (Matthew 5:15,16). Jesus himself is the true light of the world (John 8:12), and we reflect his glory. But the only way the people who walk in darkness are going to see his glory is through us; in our daily lives as joiners, plumbers, computer technicians, civil servants, housewives and so forth. We are called to live out the Christian life in the world, to say '"No" to ungodliness and worldly passions, and to live self-controlled, upright and godly lives in this present age' (Titus 2:12). We have a heavy responsibility, and it is surprising how easily we forget it.

It is important to notice that our light must shine *in order that* others see our good deeds and glorify our Father in heaven. Not that we are to strut around saying 'look at me and see how holy I am.'

Indeed, if we think of ourselves as people who are better than most at making an impression as holy people, we are probably not making much of an impression at all. Our spiritual pride will destroy our witness. But if on the other hand we make it our business to grow in Christ's likeness and not worry too much about our image, we are probably influencing others more than we think. Be that as it may, we should certainly never be satisfied with our progress. 'Do everything without complaining or arguing,' says Paul, 'so that you may become blameless and pure, children of God without fault in a crooked and depraved generation, in which you shine like stars in the universe as you hold out the word of life...' (Philippians 2:14-16). We have a long way to go!

We should also notice that deeds come before words. People must be able to *see* what we are before they will listen to what we say. Even so, unless some unforgiven sin has robbed us of our right to speak, we must not shy away from speaking a word for the Lord whenever the opportunity arises. We may not be called to be evangelists, ministers of the word, or missionaries, but we are to witness verbally nevertheless, and not to be ashamed of the gospel of Christ (Romans 1:16). If you are like me, the opportunity will not always be easy to spot and it will pass before we realise it. We need to pray for grace to be alert so that we may make the most of every opportunity when it comes.

Jesus did not mean that everyone who sees our good deeds will praise God. On the contrary, godliness often proves to be an irritation to the godless. Even if no word is spoken, a holy life stands as a challenge, and not infrequently provokes a strong reaction. A newly converted friend of mine who worked as a scaffolder, was subjected to endless taunts by his workmates as soon as they saw how his life had changed. Day after day he was persecuted in this way, so that life became almost unbearable for him. No doubt this is what Paul meant by the sufferings of Christ flowing over into our lives (2 Corinthians 1:5); the sufferings believers are called upon to endure because of our union with him. 'If the world hate you,' Jesus said, 'keep in mind that it hated me first. If you belonged to the world, it would love you as its own. As it is, you do not belong to the world, but I have chosen you out of the world. That is why the world hates you' (John 15:18). Paul too, warns us that 'everyone who wants to live a godly life in Christ Jesus will be persecuted...' (2 Timothy 3:12).

For two thousand years, Christians have been witnesses for Christ, often in face of severe persecution and, as a result, the gospel has spread throughout the world. Millions have turned to Christ – and it all began on the day of Pentecost when the Spirit was poured out on the apostles in fulfilment of the promise of Jesus: 'But you will receive power when the Holy Spirit comes on you; and you will be my witnesses in Jerusalem, and in all Judea and Samaria, and to the ends of the earth' (Acts 1:8). If the Spirit had not been given, the apostles would have remained behind locked doors trembling in fear of the Jews (John 20:19).

To be faithful witnesses for Christ is simply a matter of obedience to his command (Matthew 28:19), but how much stronger our motivation becomes as we see more and more of his glory. The power the Spirit gives us to be Christ's witnesses, is not an ability to impose ourselves on others, or to put pressure on them to 'make a decision'. It is the power to share what we know of the glory of Christ in our own experience. Like Peter and John, we find 'we cannot help speaking about what we have seen and heard' (Acts 4:20). In this way, as the Spirit reveals more of the glory of Christ *to* us, so he reveals more of the glory of Christ through us. After all, what is it we want people to see? Do we want to advertise the church? Do we want to draw attention to ourselves? Not at all. We want them to see Jesus, and if they should see him in us, then to him be the glory. Luke tells us that when the rulers, elders and teachers of the law 'saw the courage of Peter and John and realised that they were unschooled, ordinary men, they were astonished and they took note that these men had been with Jesus' (Acts 4:13). We don't know what it was that caused them to take note of the fact, but we can be sure that the boldness and sincerity of these two 'ordinary men' was sufficient in itself to show from whom they had received their training. If they had not been in such close fellowship with Jesus, the impact they made would not have been so powerful. So it should be with us. The Lord may sometimes honour the witness of the most uncommitted believer, but as a general rule, the beauty of Jesus will be seen more clearly in the lives of those who take time to be with him.

This doesn't mean that those who are young in the faith must keep their mouths shut. The preparation Jesus gives is what we might call 'in-service training'. From the moment we receive his Spirit we are his witnesses, and we learn as we go along. I like the story of the blind man in John's gospel. Here was a man who had 'been with Jesus' and had not only received his physical sight, but his spiritual sight as well. But he was still conscious of his ignorance and not ashamed to admit it. Even so, he was prepared to tell the churlish and unbelieving Pharisees exactly what he knew about Jesus. 'What have you to say about him?…' they demanded. 'The man replied, "He is a prophet." The Jews still did not believe that he had been blind and had received his sight...' and so 'A second time they summoned the man who had been blind... "Give glory to God," they said, "We know this man is a sinner." He replied, "Whether he is a sinner or not, I don't know. One thing I do know: I was blind but now I see!"' (John 9:17-18, 24-25). Just imagine – the man didn't even know whether Jesus was a sinner or not, but yet he was prepared to say what Jesus had done for him! So much for those Christians who say they cannot be witnesses for Christ because they do not know enough. I have met far too many.

3. He Baptises us into One Body

We saw just now that the promise of the Holy Spirit was first made to the apostles (Acts 1:5, 8). Luke is informing his readers of the qualifications of the apostles for the task to which God had called them. But we must not make the mistake of thinking that they were the only ones who were baptised with the Spirit, or that this was an additional blessing for some but not for others. Nor should we think of the 'power' the apostles received as being the only purpose of the outpouring of the Spirit. The Spirit was given in order that they may belong to Christ and this being so it followed inevitably that they were to be his witnesses. In other words, it was as a direct result of their union with the Lord Jesus Christ that they were given power to witness. The purpose of the gift of the Spirit was not primarily to give them power *to do* but *to be*. What they *did* was the consequence of what they *were*.

Exactly the same is true of us. If we have been baptised with the Spirit we belong to Christ and therefore we are his witnesses. If we have not been baptised with the Spirit, we do not belong to Christ and therefore we cannot be his witnesses. Obviously, we are not witnesses of the resurrection of Christ as the apostles were, but we are witnesses just the same, for the simple reason that, like the apostles, we now belong to him and have seen his glory.

For many decades now the idea that the baptism of the Spirit is a blessing believers may or may not receive *at or after* conversion, has been widely canvassed. It gives rise to some hard questions to which there is no satisfactory answer. In view of what Paul says in Romans 8:9: 'If anyone does not have the Spirit of Christ, he does not belong to Christ,' in what sense can those who have not received the Spirit be called Christians? If they are to be regarded as believers, are they called to be witnesses for Christ or not? And if the outpouring of the Spirit on the Day of Pentecost was a supplementary blessing reserved for those who fulfil certain conditions, why did *all* the apostles receive it unconditionally? And why did their testimony throughout the book of Acts focus on Christ and his redemption and not on the need for believers to receive the Spirit? (Some appeal to Acts 19:1-7, where Paul asks 'some disciples' if they received the Holy Spirit when they believed, but careful reading of the text shows that these men were not Christians because they had never heard of the Spirit. They were disciples of John the Baptist).

Most distressing of all however, is the fact that our differences centre on what is the very basis of our unity. 'The body is a unit,' says Paul, 'though it is made up of many parts; and though all its parts are many, they form one body. So it is with Christ. For we were all baptised by one Spirit into one body – whether Jews or Greeks, slave or free – and we were all given the same Spirit to drink' (1 Corinthians 12:12, 13). The repetition of the word 'all' should not be missed. The apostle is teaching that no matter how serious our previous differences were, the baptism of the Spirit has made us one. Just as every part of the human body is in harmony with every other part because all the parts partake of the same life, so now we are all united as partakers of Christ our head. Since Paul was so concerned to establish this truth as the basis of our unity in the body of Christ, how can we justify separation on the ground that we have been baptised with the Spirit and others have not?

But none of this must be taken to imply that experiences of being 'filled with the Spirit' subsequent to our initial baptism into the body of Christ, are impossible. Since God is Sovereign, it would be very foolish to try and limit the work of the Holy Spirit in this way. In any case, although the initial baptism of the Spirit is not something that can be, or need be repeated, many believers experience times of rich blessing that lift them to a higher spiritual plane altogether. It may be an empowering of the Spirit for a special task of some kind, or it may be a deeper assurance of salvation. Indeed, for those who are truly born of the Spirit, but who, through their negligence, are still 'infants in Christ' (1 Corinthians 3:1), such times of blessing are already long overdue. But when such a personal revival takes place, it must not be confused with the baptism of the Spirit and not regarded as such. Nor must it be seen as the norm for all believers. God deals with us all differently, and it is sheer folly to think of *my* spiritual experience as a pattern for everyone else. What often happens is that believers who have genuine experiences of the Spirit after their conversion, assume that this is the 'baptism of the Spirit' they have been told about. That is to say their experience may well be genuine, but their theology is false.

Of course, there is much more to our divisions that this. In more recent times further disharmony has been caused over the matter of prostrations, physical contortions, and the loss of self-control (even in the presence of unbelievers) which are stoutly defended as the work of the Spirit of God. It must be evident however, even to those who approve of these things, that attempts to find support in the word of God have met with no success. I read an article in a recent issue of the *Renewal* magazine in which the writer tried to use Scripture to defend the practice of making animal noises while under the alleged influence of the Spirit. He failed miserably. Using some words from the prophet Micah, 'I will howl like a jackal,' and without even looking at the context, he insisted that this was sufficient to prove the point! The full text reads: 'Because of this I will weep and wail; I will go barefoot and naked. I will howl like a jackal and moan like an owl. For her wound is incurable...' (Micah 1:8, 9). The prophet selected the two creatures that make the most mournful noises during the night to add colour to his moving expression of grief. He is lamenting the sins of God's people. What connection can there be between a meaningful lament over sin and a meaningless mimicking of animals? The writer's uncertainty about the validity of his argument was exposed at the end of the article, when he questioned the need to have biblical warrant for everything we do anyway? If our divisions are to be healed, we really must stop abusing the Scriptures in this way.

Others have seized on Paul's words in Ephesians 5:18 to defend such practices: 'Do not get drunk on wine, which leads to debauchery. Instead, be filled with the Spirit.' We don't need to be reminded what people are like when they get drunk. Some are abusive; some are merry (if that is not a misuse of the word) and some fall about and make complete fools of themselves. But what comparison can there be between this and being filled with the Spirit? Again, careful reading of the context will show that the apostle is making a contrast, not a comparison. Being filled with wine leads to debauchery, but being filled with the Spirit leads to praise and worship. Those

who are under the influence of the Spirit do not lose control of themselves; on the contrary, the Spirit controls their thoughts and actions
in a manner that honours Christ.

This must surely be obvious when we consider that self-control
is named as one of the fruits of the Spirit (Galatians 5:22). How can
he be the author of experiences that cause people to lose consciousness or to lose control of themselves and behave in an undignified
manner? There is no evidence whatsoever in Scripture that people
behaved in this way under the influence of the Holy Spirit or when
the apostles laid hands on them.

The continuing emphasis on the feel good factor has now brought
us to the point where people who have little or no understanding of
the faith, but have had a 'spiritual' experience of some kind, are
accepted as new converts in the church. As a result there is now
disagreement over the question as to what a Christian is. That such
an extreme point should be reached among evangelicals is surely an
indication that we have lost our way.

For years, the so-called 'ecumaniacs' – church people who press
for the merging of denominations in the conviction that this will
answer Christ's prayer for unity – have been claiming that the exist-
ence of different church organisations is a scandal. But what Jesus
prayed for is not the unity of different organisations (they did not
exist in his time), but a unity of true believers. Disunity among those
who love the Lord and believe his word is far more serious than the
failure to bring about schemes of reunion between the various
denominations. It divides churches, separates friends, and introduces
tensions into Christian families. It sends out a confusing message
and seriously damages the church's witness.

It is my conviction – a conviction that gave rise to the writing of
this book – that if this subjectivism were to be replaced with a
passion for the glory of Christ, a hunger for the word of God, and an
eagerness to grow in holiness, our current divisions would soon be a
thing of the past. In our fascination with the work of the Spirit we
seem to have forgotten that he is the Spirit of unity. Our failure to

'keep the unity of the Spirit through the bond of peace' (Ephesians 4:3), grieves him deeply (Ephesians 4:30). So if, instead of seeking further 'blessings' for ourselves – experiences that separate us from others – we took the time to search the Scriptures, remembering always that the Spirit is our teacher, we would more readily acknowledge that in Christ we have absolutely everything. We would be the more able to rejoice that 'in Christ all the fulness of the Deity lives in bodily form,' and that we 'have been given fulness in Christ' (Colossians 2:9,10). We would also know much more about that fellowship of which John speaks – fellowship with the Father and the Son, and with one another (1 John 1:3). What a difference that would make in our testimony!

In the light of his prayer to his Father, I sometimes wonder what the Lord Jesus feels about us: 'I have given them the glory that you gave me, that they may be one as we are one: I in them and you in me. May they be brought to complete unity to let the world know that you sent me and loved them even as you have loved me' (John 17:22, 23). Jesus is here praying for *all* believers (his prayer would not make any sense otherwise). To be united with Christ is the glory of *every* believer. Through him we are *all* partakers of *all* the blessings, purchased for us with his precious blood, This is the reason why we are all one in him (Galatians 3:28). This, said Jesus, is what convinces an unbelieving world.

The Life of Faith

CHAPTER SIX

Seeing Jesus by Faith

'Therefore we are always confident and know that as long as we are at home in the body we are away from the Lord. We live by faith, not by sight' (2 Corinthians 5: 6, 7).

1. The Function of Faith

My wife and I are frequent visitors to the town of Scarborough, which is only a few miles from our home. From the Esplanade – a road that runs on top of the cliff – there is a commanding view over the bay. It takes in the harbour, the lighthouse, and the castle. A number of seats are provided for public use, each one being donated in memory of someone who has died. The inscription on one of the seats simply says, 'Enjoy the View. I did.'

Not long ago, as we sat on one of these seats, a sea mist had rolled in. We could just see the harbour, the faint outline of the castle, and the tiny and indistinct figures of people on the beach. In these circumstances we were able to enjoy the view to some extent, but our appreciation increased as the sun became stronger and the mist slowly dispersed.

The view we now have of the glory of Christ cannot compare with the glory to be revealed when the mist has cleared away, and we see him as he is in all his glory. But it can still be thoroughly enjoyed, not least because we know that soon the great day will dawn when faith gives way to sight. By faith, we see but a poor reflection and although it should be improving all the time, it will always leave a lot to be desired. How could it be otherwise when, in the nature of the case, our faith anticipates the perfect sight of Christ in his transcendent glory, and the transformation of our lives into his likeness?

A friend of mine strongly disapproves of Christians who say they 'live by faith.' Their faith, he complains, is always well advertised and some do very well out of it. He is thinking of course, of people who have no fixed income and claim to trust the Lord to provide the necessities of life. But when the apostle Paul wrote about living by faith this is certainly not what he meant.

Another example of the way in which faith is misunderstood was provided by my local church secretary recently when he announced in church that there would be a 'faith tea'. 'If you are coming,' he said, 'please bring something with you – a quiche, a pizza, or a trifle – something of that sort.' Whenever these so-called 'faith teas' are held there is always a plentiful supply of food, because all who come feel a duty to give something towards it. To say it is 'living by faith' is bordering on the ridiculous.

'Living by faith' is not what some Christians do; nor is it what all Christians do sometimes. It is what all Christians do, all the time. If we do not live by faith we are not Christians. Our salvation is a future possession (Romans 13:11) that we cannot see, except with the eye of faith, and we go forward trusting in the promises of God. We shall go on living by faith as long as we live in this world. True faith cannot fail for two reasons:

First, God is faithful and therefore he will not – indeed he cannot – go back on his promise to give eternal life to all who truly believe. Augustus Toplady (1740-78) puts it well:

> The work which his goodness began,
> the arm of his strength will complete;
> His promise is Yes and Amen,
> and never was forfeited yet.

Second, since God has given us saving faith – faith that secures salvation – we cannot fail to inherit eternal life. It is for this reason that the writer to the Hebrews defines faith as 'being sure of what we hope for and certain of what we do not see' (Hebrews 11:1).

But as we saw earlier, our faith is not only in a promise, but a person. The promises of Scripture, together with all its teaching are vitally important of course, because without the written word we would know nothing about the living Word. We cannot trust in Jesus unless we know what the Scripture says about him. But here lies the danger; it is possible to know about Jesus and to believe the promises in our heads without knowing him as a person. Without this personal relationship, our 'faith' is merely intellectual, amounting to nothing more than accepting information in the mind. If this is the case with us, we are still strangers to the grace of God. Sad to say, this is as far as many church people get. They believe the creeds in the head but do not know Christ in the heart. They do not understand that truth *about* Jesus cannot convey grace, mercy and forgiveness to us. It is Christ and Christ alone who is our life (Colossians 3:4).

The Bible teaches that true faith is the gift of God, and that by faith, we who were by nature objects of wrath are made 'alive with Christ … in order that in the coming ages he might show the incomparable riches of his grace expressed in his kindness to us in Christ Jesus' (Ephesians 2:5, 7). All our spiritual blessings come to us through a personal and living relationship with him. And not least of these blessings is the ability to look forward with joy to the day when we shall see his glory with our own eyes.

The temptation to look back must therefore be resisted. The only exception to this is the duty we have to remember the pit out of which we were rescued by the grace of God (Ephesians 2:11-13). Some believers tend to look back too much because they are taken up with the idea that their relationship with Jesus would have been better if they had been privileged, as the disciples were, to walk and talk with him. I mention this because the idea was put into my mind as a child through some of the hymns we used to sing in Sunday School. The following words come to mind:

> I wish that his hand had been placed on my head,
> That his arms had been thrown around me,
> And that I might have seen his kind look when he said,
> 'Let the little ones come unto me.'
> *Jemima Luke (1813-1906).*

If the disciples were better off than we are, why would Jesus tell them that it was for their good that he was leaving them? 'Unless I go away' he said, 'the Counsellor will not come to you' (John 16:7). The Counsellor (or Comforter) is 'the Spirit of truth' who will testify about Jesus (John 15:26); the one of whom Jesus said: 'He will bring glory to me by taking from what is mine and making it known to you' (John 16:14). It was good therefore for the disciples that Jesus was leaving them because without the Holy Spirit they would never have had 'the full riches of complete understanding' (Colossians 2:2). We too have the precious gift of the Spirit, and he reveals Jesus to us through the faithful testimony and teaching of the apostles. We are therefore capable of growing in faith faster than the disciples were before the events of Easter and Pentecost. Even if we had been able to rub shoulders with Jesus, what glory would we have seen in him without the enlightenment of the Spirit? After all, there was nothing attractive in his human appearance or his earthly status, as the prophet Isaiah foretold: 'He had no beauty or majesty to attract us to him, nothing in his appearance that we should desire him' (Isaiah 53:2).

The people of Nazareth where Jesus grew up were with him all the time and yet they saw nothing in him. When he began teaching them in their synagogue, they were amazed, and said: '"Is this not Jesus, the son of Joseph, whose father and mother we know. How can he now say, 'I came down from heaven?"' (John 6:42). '"Where did this man get this wisdom and these miraculous powers?" …And they took offence at him' (Matthew 13:54-57). Had we been in their shoes, our attitude would have been much the same, 'for the god of this age has blinded the minds of unbelievers, so that they cannot see the light of the gospel of the glory of Christ, who is the image of God' (2 Corinthians 4:4). But now, through the Scriptures, the glory of Christ they are unable to see, is revealed to us by the Spirit. Why God should be merciful to us in this way is beyond our understanding.

No doubt some will be quick to point out that Peter, James and John saw the glory of Jesus on the Mount of Transfiguration with their own eyes and therefore they must have been more privileged than we are. The veil over Christ's glory was lifted briefly and 'His face shone like the sun, and his clothes became white as light' (Matthew 17:2). The three disciples also saw Moses and Elijah in their 'glorious splendour' talking with him (Luke 9:28-33). Certainly the three disciples were privileged to have a brief sight of the transcendent glory of Christ which we cannot yet have, but when we read the story carefully, we see that they were totally unprepared and ill equipped to cope with it. The full significance of the event did not dawn on them until later (2 Peter 1:16-18). At the time, Peter and his companions were half asleep and didn't know what was going on, and even when they became fully awake it appears they were not thinking straight. Luke tells us that Peter did not know what he was talking about when, as impulsive as ever, he suggested that three shelters should be built, one for Jesus, one for Moses, and one for Elijah. And finally, when he and his companions heard the voice from heaven, 'they fell face down to the ground, terrified' (Matthew 17:6).

Some think the apostle John was referring to this event when he said: 'We have seen his glory, the glory of the one and only Son, who came from the Father, full of grace and truth (John 1:14). But we cannot be sure about this, especially in view of John's description of Christ's glory as being 'full of grace and truth.' These words do not fit easily into John's experience on the Mount of Transfiguration, and he is therefore more likely to be thinking of the splendour of Christ's character seen in his words and deeds. John's meaning seems to be: 'We observed Jesus and listened to him throughout his ministry, and we perceived his glory.' Whatever view we take, the experience of the disciples on the Mount could not have given them a more mature, or a more settled, view of Christ's glory than we may have by faith. With the added benefit of the apostolic writings, we have the privilege of seeing more and more of his glory. What a shame we don't make more use of it!

Moreover, the glory of Jesus revealed to the disciples and many of their contemporaries was perceived by faith, just as it is with us. Without the gift of faith they would have seen nothing in Jesus; and with the gift of faith they saw nothing that we cannot also see. The Lord Jesus chose to reveal his glory to us, just as he did to them. When he performed the miracle of turning the water into wine for example, John tells us that; 'He thus revealed his glory, and his disciples put their faith in him' (John 2:11). This cannot mean that this was the first time the disciples had believed. The first chapter of John's Gospel shows that their eyes were being opened before this. John is saying that as a result of the miracle, their faith in him was strengthened. But nor can it mean that since we did not witness the miracle, our faith in Christ and our awareness of his power are adversely affected.

Broadly speaking, we could say there are three stages in the revelation of Christ's glory to his people that could be described as good, better, and best. The revelation made to us at our conversion was partial but good. The revelation made to us as we grow in grace and see more of his glory through the Scriptures is still partial but better. Finally, the revelation of his glory when we see him face to face will be no longer partial and therefore will be by far the best. Obviously, the distance between stage two and three is much greater than it is between stage one and two.

During my years in the jewellery trade, my appreciation of the beauty and value of diamonds gradually increased, not least because more and more high quality stones came into my hands. At least, this was the case, until one day I had an experience that changed everything. I shall never forget it. One of my responsibilities was to value articles left for repair, this valuation being entered on a form of agreement signed by the customer. This figure was the limit of our liability should the article be lost or stolen. On this memorable day, a lady came into the shop asking for the clasp on a brooch to be repaired. It was made up of two overlapping circles of gems with about twelve stones in each. I knew that one of the circles was set with blue sapphires, but what were the others? It is probably true to say that at first sight I knew they were diamonds, but the colour, brightness, and clarity of the stones was such that I could not believe what I was seeing, especially as there were so many. I had never seen diamonds like them. Looking back on it afterwards, I scolded myself for not trusting my own judgement, but in the event my hesitation caused to me to put a low value on the article. The fact that the lady signed the agreement without a murmur tended to confirm my doubts. After she had gone, I consulted someone with more experience and he confirmed that they were flawless blue-white diamonds of about one carat each. From that day forward, in the light of their breathtaking beauty, my appreciation of poorer quality diamonds waned. This incident took place well over forty years ago, and yet those diamonds are still sparkling in my mind!

Apart from the fact that the flaws are in us and not in Christ, this is how it is with our progression through faith from the first day Jesus was revealed to us to the day we see him face to face in all his beauty. What we see in him today affords such pleasure that it bears no comparison with the view we had of him in the past, when our faith and understanding were weaker. But when we see him in all his glory and perfection with our own eyes, what we knew of him by faith will seem insignificant by comparison. The sight will be totally and immediately transforming.

The prominence given to faith must not be taken to imply that reason is not important. The contrast in Scripture is between faith and sight, not between faith and reason. Although faith goes beyond reason in the sense that there are many truths we believe but can not explain, it does not mean that faith is unreasonable. Jesus himself, when encouraging his hearers not to be anxious about life's necessities, told them to use their reason. Look at the birds and the flowers, he said, and *think*. The birds 'do not sow or reap or store away in barns, and yet your heavenly Father feeds them…' 'See how the lilies of the field grow. They do not labour or spin. Yet I tell you that not even Solomon in all his splendour was dressed like one of these. If that is how God clothes the grass of the field, which is here today and tomorrow is thrown into the fire, will he not much more clothe you, O you of little faith?' (Matthew 6:26-30). Christians need to *think* more. We need to gain as much knowledge as we can. Knowledge is very useful and poses no threat to our faith. Like money, the only thing we need to watch is our attitude to it. If we become proud of our knowledge we are in grave danger. So let us learn all we can, always keeping in mind that the most unlearned believer will see more of the glory of Christ than the most learned unbeliever. Faith is 'the evidence of things not seen' (Hebrews 11:1) in the sense that what is not evident to our natural reason alone, however well developed, is clearly evident to the eye of faith.

How precious then is God's gift of faith! It enables us to explore the great mystery whereby Christ assumed our nature in order to redeem it. It opens our eyes to see the glory of Jesus who became man without ceasing to be God; finite and mortal, yet infinite and immortal! And for what purpose? So that in this life we who are made in the image and glory of God (1 Corinthians 11:7) but have become vile and mortal, may be refined by grace and made ready to share his glory forever in a redeemed and renewed universe.

2. The Eye of Faith

When I was a child, I was always amused by the tale of the blind man who said 'I see' and then walked into a lamp post! The man had no physical sight, but he was able to understand. We might say he had no sight but he did have insight. In everyday speech, when we say 'I see' we simply mean we understand; we follow the logic of a particular statement. Now I wonder if such a man in real life would change places with another who had sight, but no insight. I think not. Physical sight is a very precious gift, but surely the gift of insight is more precious. A blind man with understanding is surely better off than a sighted man with none. People who are 'ever seeing but never perceiving, and ever hearing but never understanding' (Mark 4:12) have a fatal handicap.

So when we talk about 'seeing' Jesus by faith, we simply mean we have God-given insight regarding his glorious Person. We understand the truth about him. In this context, the word 'understanding' takes on a new meaning. It is not only comprehending the meaning of words, but knowing the truth of them in the heart as well. And by the word 'heart' we do not refer to the muscle that pumps blood around the body, but to the inner self – what we sometimes call the soul. It is an experiential knowledge. When my wife says 'I love you,' I not only understand the meaning of the words in my head – which does not affect me much; I also know their meaning in my heart – and that affects me deeply. In the same way, there is all the difference in the world between understanding in my head what the Bible says about the love of Christ, which changes nothing, and knowing that love in my heart, which changes everything. Paul's prayer in Ephesians 3:17-19 expresses it well: 'And I pray that you, being rooted and established in love, may have power, together with all the saints, to grasp how wide and long and high and deep is the love of Christ, and to know this love that surpasses knowledge – that you may be filled to the measure of all the fulness of God.'

The same is true of the word 'mind' as it is used in several places in the Bible. For example, when Jesus opened the minds of his disciples to understand the Scriptures (Luke 24:45), he was not just feeding them with information. The knowledge he gave them illuminated their whole being. Similarly, when Paul exhorts his readers to 'be transformed by the renewing of your mind' (Romans 12:2), he is thinking of a complete change of heart and life.

The opposite of an enlightened heart (or mind) is a darkened heart. Speaking of the godless, Paul says 'their thinking became futile and their foolish hearts were darkened.' (Romans 1:21). Darkened hearts and foolish thinking always go together. The apostle John, in his writings, uses the words 'darkness' and 'light' in a similar way. 'Light' stands for the knowledge of Christ and 'darkness' for ignorance and sin. In this sense Jesus is 'the light of the world' (John 8:12). He is the only one through whom the light of glory shines. So when John says: 'The light shines in the darkness, but the darkness has not understood it' (John 1:5), he means that the ignorance of sinful men prevents them from knowing Jesus. As we said a moment ago, such understanding is reserved for those to whom God gives the gift of faith. 'I have come into the world as a light' Jesus said, 'so that no one who believes in me should stay in darkness' (John 12:46).

So when the writer to the Hebrews exhorts us to 'fix our eyes on Jesus' he is thinking about the 'eyes of your heart' (Ephesians 1:18); the eyes of the understanding. And since it is by faith that his glory is revealed, we may also speak of seeing Jesus with the 'eye of faith.' The light that now shines in our hearts is 'the light of the *knowledge* of the glory of God in the face of Christ' (2 Corinthians 4: 6). God illuminates our minds through the Scriptures so that we apprehend and appreciate his glory.

Our primary duty then, if we have the gift of faith, is to keep the glory of Christ constantly in view. Our ability to do this is one of the greatest privileges God has conferred upon unworthy sinners and it is by means of this privilege that we grow into the likeness of Christ. All the passing pleasures of this world cannot compare with the ever-increasing joy we experience as we look to him. No matter how much we enjoy the delights of this life, they will fade; but our vision of Christ by faith is something that gets better by the day. The more we contemplate his glory, the more we appreciate his beauty. And as we grow older, we become more and more captivated by it. At least, that's how it should be.

If we are looking to Jesus, we shall always have a deep desire to know him better. If it is not so with us, and we really want to see Jesus more clearly (and thereby learn to love him more dearly), we really must pray for grace to develop the discipline of fixing our eyes on the Christ of the Scriptures.

This function of faith is not merely for personal satisfaction; it sets the standard for our lives. The blessing comes, not in the view, but in the deed. In any case, a clearer view of him *depends* on our obedience to his word. James invites us to think of a mirror as illustrating the right use of God's word. We are to look into it regularly and take care we do not forget what it tells us about ourselves, for 'the man who looks intently in the perfect law that gives freedom, and continues to do so, not forgetting what he has heard, but doing it – he will be blessed in what he does' (James 1:25).

Therefore, the more we 'walk in the light as he is in the light' (1 John 1:7), the more we shall grow into his likeness, and the better equipped we shall be to take up the cross and follow him (Matthew 10:38). We shall also be better equipped to cope with the trials and temptations of life, from which there is no escape. Severe trials may cause the strongest believer's faith to waver for a time. Indeed, God may call us to go through times of trial so severe that we begin to wonder if he has forsaken us altogether. During these times we may find it hard to keep Jesus in our view. For this reason we must be sure to fix our eyes on him during the good times, so that we shall be better able to endure the trial when it comes, and to recover our confidence quickly when it has passed. The Christian virtues of patience, perseverance and endurance do not grow any other way. So 'consider it pure joy, my brothers, whenever you face trials of many kinds, because you know that the testing of your faith develops perseverance…' (James 1:2, 3). 'We do not want you to become lazy, but to imitate those who through faith and patience inherit what has been promised' (Hebrews 6:12).

Jesus is our supreme example of faith because as he endured the suffering of the cross, he kept his eye on 'the joy set before him'. This is the reason why the writer to the Hebrews urges us to do the same: 'Therefore...let us throw off everything that hinders and the sin that so easily entangles, and let us run with perseverance the race marked out for us. Let us fix our eyes on Jesus, the author and Perfecter of our faith, who for the joy set before him endured the cross, scorning its shame, and sat down at the right hand of the throne of God' (Hebrews 12:1, 2). A similar command is given in 3: 1: 'Therefore holy brothers, who share in the heavenly calling, fix your thoughts on Jesus, the apostle and high priest whom we confess.' Here the readers are exhorted to contemplate the glory of Christ as mediator of the new covenant. (The words 'fix your thoughts' have the same meaning as 'fix your eyes').

3. The Limitations of Faith

The apostle Paul also uses a mirror as an illustration of the limitations of faith. When we look into the near perfect mirrors of today, we feel as though we are looking *through* the glass. We get the impression that the reflected image is really in front of us. This is why modern floor to ceiling mirrors are so dangerous. People do not see the mirror and so they walk into it. The mirrors of Paul's day however, were of poor quality and therefore gave a poor reflection. But the apostle goes on to say that when perfection comes, 'we shall see face to face. Now I know in part; then shall I know fully, even as I am fully known' (1 Corinthians 13:12).

One of the reasons why our vision is blurred is that we are afflicted by doubts. They invade our thoughts without warning. When this happens, we immediately scold ourselves, and it is helpful to remember that such spontaneous disapproval proves that we are living by faith. Those who are devoid of faith are not a bit troubled by their unbelief. As we grow stronger in the faith, these doubts should afflict us less and less. Contemplating the glory of Christ in the Scriptures is the best cure for doubts. Such contemplation will also help us to see material and temporal things in their true light and weaken our attachment to them. It will strengthen our endurance, stimulate holy living, and put a restraint on the plaintive spirit. 'He alone' says John Calvin, 'has made solid progress in the gospel who has acquired the habit of meditating continually on a blessed resurrection' (*Institutes,* book 3, chapter 25).

Today, many believers are attracted by the idea that if we have enough faith, we need not depend on the Bible so much. They think there are better and perhaps easier ways of knowing the mind of God. Why should we not have further prophecies and revelations that will improve our knowledge of Jesus? After all, the Bible is dated and we need to know what God is saying today. But this is sheer folly. To try to add to God's word is a sure way of making shipwreck of our faith. None of us would accept the claim of the Mormons that the Bible is incomplete without the revelations made to Joseph Smith in the nineteenth century (the Book of Mormon). Why then should we encourage the notion that further revelations are necessary? When two Mormon gentlemen came to my door recently and tried to defend the revelation made to Joseph Smith, was I not right to point them to Hebrews 1:1: 'In the past God spoke to our forefathers through the prophets at many times and in various ways, but in these last days he has spoken to us by his Son'? The writer is saying that the revelation of Jesus given to the apostles and recorded in Holy Writ is God's final word. Nothing can be added; and nothing need be added.

4. The Blessings of Faith

In my early Christian life I suffered much at the hands of well-meaning believers who urged me to seek further blessings. I vividly remember a well-meaning Christian woman saying to me: 'Just as you received Christ by faith, you must now seek the second blessing of entire sanctification by faith.' Other equally sincere people urged me to seek the blessing of perfect rest, or the baptism of the Spirit. Sadly, it was some years before I realised the serious nature of their error. They did not realise that all the fulness of God dwells in Christ (Colossians 1:19) and that in him 'are hidden all the treasures of wisdom and knowledge' (Colossians 2:3). It is therefore impossible to have blessings that supplement Christ. To have him is to have everything. This does not mean that there are not treasures of wisdom and knowledge hidden away that we have not yet found. The riches of Christ are unsearchable, inexhaustible, but they are all ours (Ephesians 3:8).

It is important then, for every believer to understand that all spiritual blessings are in Christ and they are ours as a consequence of our union with him. Christ meets all our need, and by faith he dwells in our hearts in all his fulness. The apostle Paul warned his readers of the danger of the idea that to have Christ is not enough and insisted that 'in Christ all the fulness of the Deity lives in bodily form, and you have been given fulness in Christ...' (Colossians 2:9, 10). The false teachers of his day were claiming that further experiences and observances were necessary in order to be a complete Christian. But the fulness of God is not the special blessing of some privileged believers; it is the possession of all who are united to Christ.

Notice how Paul uses the past tense in Ephesians 1:3: 'Praise be to the God and Father of our Lord Jesus Christ, who has blessed us in the heavenly realms with every spiritual blessing in Christ.' The past tense is used because the apostle thinks of his readers as already in possession of all these blessings. Christ has purchased them for us. Paul goes on to show that this was according to the sovereign will of God from past eternity. And until the day when we fully realise these blessings, he who is seated at the right hand of God 'dwells in our hearts through faith' (Ephesians 3:17) by his Spirit. He shields us by his power 'until the coming of the salvation to be revealed in the last time' (1 Peter 1:5). What more can we ask?

CHAPTER SEVEN

The Hope of Glory

1. What is Christian Hope?
2. The Realization of Hope
3. Rejoicing in Hope
4. The Patience of Hope
5. The Encouragement of Hope
6. What Are We Hoping For?

'But we ought always to thank God for you, brothers loved by the Lord, because from the beginning God chose you to be saved through the sanctifying work of the Spirit and through belief in the truth. He called you to this through our gospel, that you might share in the glory of our Lord Jesus Christ' (2 Thessalonians 2:13, 14).

1. What is Christian Hope?

In the United States of America, a 'hope-chest' is a box in which a woman, hoping to get married, keeps the things she will need. In England, it would be called a 'bottom drawer'. But what if the lady has no suitor? Or if she has, what if he changes his mind? All sorts of things could happen to prevent her hopes being realised.

Many people think Christians are in a similar situation when they talk about their hope of eternal life. We may realise the hope or we may not, and there is no way of knowing. We can hardly blame them for getting this impression, because the word 'hope', as it is used in everyday conversation, always has an air of uncertainty about it. Sometimes, the basis of the 'hope' people entertain is so shaky, it can be no more than a wish. Take the lottery for example; people purchase their tickets in the hope of winning the jackpot but the chances are less than one in a million.

Recently, my wife and I planned to go away for a few days holiday, but some weeks before our departure I fell sick. When my friends asked me if I would be well enough to take the break, I could only reply: 'I hope so.' My use of the word 'hope' in this context was an admission that I may be disappointed. In fact, I felt so ill, my hopes were fading fast.

This air of uncertainty is evident in the way the word 'hope' is used in many places in the Bible. For example, Paul tells the Christians in Rome that he hopes to visit them on his way to Spain (Romans 15:24), but his visit is by no means certain. In the event, his hope of visiting them was realised, but not as he expected. He arrived in Rome, not on his way to Spain, but as the prisoner of Caesar. We find the same meaning in 1 Corinthians 9:10: '…when the ploughman ploughs and the thresher threshes, they ought to do so in the hope of sharing in the harvest.' But the harvest may fail.

When the word is used to refer to the expectation of the glory to come however, there is nothing uncertain about it. It is based on a solid foundation. The distinction frequently made in common speech between 'expectation' and 'hope', as in the phrase, 'more in hope than expectation', cannot apply to the believer's glorious inheritance. 'We have this hope as an anchor for the soul, firm and secure' (Hebrews: 6:19). Here the writer pictures our life in this world as a ship in a stormy sea and our hope as an immovable anchor that ensures we shall never founder. An old hymn takes up the theme:

> We have an anchor that keeps the soul
> steadfast and sure while the billows roll;
> fastened to the Rock which cannot move,
> grounded firm and deep in the Saviour's love!
> *Priscilla Jane Owens (1829-99).*

One more example will suffice. Paul tells the Colossian Christians that although God's purpose to reveal the gospel to the Gentiles was hidden 'for ages and generations', the mystery has now been made known to the saints: 'To them God has chosen to make known among the Gentiles the glorious riches of this mystery, which is Christ in you, the hope of glory' (Colossians 1:27). What an astonishing truth this is! The Lord Jesus Christ, living in us by his Spirit, gives us an infallible hope of the glory to come. His presence with us is the pledge that our hope shall not fail. The light of his glory is already shining in our hearts so that we are able to look with confidence to the day when we shall be glorified together with him (2 Thessalonians 1:10).

God's promises in Christ make up the unshakeable foundation on which our hope rests and this is why we are confident of the glory to come. Let Paul explain: 'Paul, a servant of God and an apostle of Jesus Christ for the faith of God's elect and the knowledge of the truth that leads to godliness – a faith and knowledge resting on the hope of eternal life, which God, who does not lie, promised before the beginning of time...' (Titus 1:1, 2). Before the years began to roll, God promised the gift of everlasting life to his elect, those who were given by the Father to the Son in order that they might be the beneficiaries of his redemption and share his eternal glory (John 17:24). Since his promise cannot fail, nothing can prevent the hope being realised. Centuries before Paul, David expressed the same confidence: 'No one whose hope is in you (the Lord) will ever be put to shame' (Psalm 25:3). Nothing in the universe is more certain than the hope of a believer.

There is a difference however, between the certainty of our future glory, and being sure of it ourselves. So what should a Christian do if he is not fully persuaded? Before we answer the question, we should understand that to doubt our salvation is to doubt God's word, and for those who belong to Christ this is a dishonourable thing to do. We need to remember that doubting Christ is the very sin of which the world is convicted by the Holy Spirit (John 16:9) as we saw earlier. It is an affront to the faithfulness of God. 'Anyone who does not believe God' says John, 'has made him out to be a liar' (1 John 5:10).

If there is no other known sin of which we have not repented, we can be fairly sure that our insecurity is due to a lack of diligence –

neglect of the word and prayer, staying away from worship and fellowship (Hebrews 10:25). Therefore it is by giving more attention to these duties that we shall grow in confidence. Many believers need to take to heart the advice of Hebrews 6:10, 11. The writer was concerned about the lack of assurance in the hearts of his readers. He admired the way they showed their love and practical concern for each other in public but sadly, they were not showing the same concern for the building up of their own faith in private. Note the words well: 'God is not unjust; he will not forget your work and the love you have shown him as you have helped his people and continue to help them. We want each of you to show this same diligence to the very end, in order to make your hope sure.' Obviously, the writer did not want them to stop showing their love in this practical way, but he was concerned that they should also be equally determined to strengthen their personal assurance.

We hear a lot about the importance of being doers of the word, not just hearers, and it is right that we should. But we are seldom reminded about the opposite failure of being so busy *doing* that we forget the importance of our own spiritual well-being. The quality of the former is inevitably adversely affected by the neglect of the latter. This was Martha's problem. Luke tells us that she 'was distracted by all the preparations that had to be made' but her sister Mary was taking full advantage of the Lord's presence and was sitting at his feet 'listening to what he said'. Feeling under pressure, and irritated by the fact that her sister was doing nothing to help, Martha complained to the Lord: '"Lord don't you care that my sister has left me to do the work by myself? Tell her to help me!" "Martha, Martha," the Lord answered, "you are worried and upset about many things, but only one thing is needed. Mary has chosen what is better, and it will not be taken away from her"' (Luke 10:40-42). The one thing Martha needed was to sit at the feet of Jesus and learn from him, just as her sister was doing. Jesus was giving no encouragement to Mary to be lazy or inconsiderate; he was commending her for having her priorities right.

Our activity can easily become a means of silencing an uneasy conscience about our slackness in private devotion. In the short term, we may succeed in convincing ourselves that all is well, and our image as practical and caring Christians may be admired by many, but the shrivelling devotion it conceals will take its toll sooner or later. We see a parallel here in those preachers who are accused of writing in the margin of their sermon notes: 'Argument weak; shout loud.' The accusation is made in jest of course. But there is nothing humorous about those believers who work on what we might call the Martha principle: 'Devotion weak, work hard.' Nothing of value is achieved; only more frustration perhaps. When it comes to strengthening our hope, activity is no substitute for diligence in study, prayer and meditation.

I invited a near neighbour to a meeting in my home. She is a regular churchgoer and always busy doing things to help others. Her reaction, as soon as she realised she was being invited to a Bible-study meeting, was immediate and disapproving. With an unmistakable note of irritation in her voice, she said: 'That's not *my* scene, I'm a doer!' I suspected at once that her 'doing' was not the consequence of a commitment to Christ, but rather a substitute for it. Subsequently my suspicions were confirmed.

Those who think this is a harsh criticism do not realise how harmful the neglect of daily communion with God is to our spiritual health. Of course, the opposite sin of being hearers only is just as harmful, but certainly not more so. It is only by 'sitting at the feet of Jesus' that we shall see more of his glory and learn to appreciate the privilege of being the children of God. And only by the same means shall we be able to strengthen our hope of the glory to come.

In Romans 8:30, Paul uses the word 'glorified' in the past tense, as though our likeness to Jesus were already accomplished: 'And those he predestined, he also called; those he called, he also justified; those he justified, he also glorified.' He does this because the blessings of predestination, calling, justification and glorification, all come in one package. They cannot be separated. If God has predestined us to be conformed to the likeness of Christ, how can there be any doubt that he will accomplish his purpose? If therefore, we have the assurance that we have been called and justified, we should also have the assurance that we are predestined to be glorified. The importance of this assurance is stressed in the apostolic writings. Take for example, Paul's prayer that his readers may be enlightened, in order that they may *know* the hope to which he has called them, the riches of his glorious inheritance in the saints... (Ephesians 1:18); and Peter's direction to his readers to be 'all the more eager to make your calling and election sure' (2 Peter 1:10), by which he means being sure of it in themselves.

It is important to notice in passing that the word 'called', as it is used in Paul's letters, is not a general invitation that goes out to everyone; it is the particular calling of God to those whom he chooses; a calling which always guarantees a positive response. In the King James Version of the Gospels, a distinction is made between being called and being chosen, the word 'called' meaning 'invited'. We see the distinction clearly in the words of Jesus: 'For many are called, but few are chosen' (Matthew 22:14). Many are invited but many refuse the invitation. In Pauline usage, it is the 'chosen' who are called, and not one of them fails to heed the call.

From what has been said, it will be evident that hope and faith are closely related. Where one exists, so does the other. We have already noted that 'faith' is defined as 'being sure of what we hope for' (Hebrews 11:1). Therefore, anyone who claims to have faith but has no hope of eternal life is deceiving himself. It is obvious that if faith accepts the promise of God to give eternal life to all who believe, the hope of glory is bound to follow. That is to say, since faith accepts that God has already given us eternal life according to his promise (John 5:24), it follows that we shall look forward to the enjoyment of it. Conversely, if we do not have this hope, it proves that we do not believe the promise, which in turn means we are not Christians. So close is this link between faith and hope that they are sometimes joined together in the apostolic writings, as when Peter

says: 'Through him' (Christ) 'you believed in God, who raised him
from the dead and glorified him, and so your faith and hope are in
God' (1 Peter 1:21).

I once took on the rather heavy responsibility of buying a house
on behalf of an absent friend. Trusting me implicitly, he insisted that
I should go ahead and clinch the deal. To my relief, however, he was
able to view the property before signing the contract, but had he not
been able to do so, he would have possessed the title deeds to a
house he had never seen. His faith in me was such that his hope of
possessing the actual property would have been based entirely on
my trustworthiness. It is fascinating to notice that some Greek scholars
think that the words of Hebrews 11:1: 'faith is being sure of what
we hope for,' would be better translated: 'faith is the title-deed of
things hoped for.'[1] As our trust is in the promises of God, whose
word cannot fail because he cannot deny himself, our 'hope' acts
like a title deed to our home in heaven, given freely to us by the
Father, and therefore providing all the security we need.

Hope, like faith, is the gift of God. It originates in him alone. It
has nothing to do with our ability. The person with the highest intelligence has no advantage over the person with the least. Nor has it
anything to do with our circumstances; it makes no difference whether
we are rich or poor, black or white. It has everything to do with
God's sovereign will.

2. The Realization of Hope

The beauty of those diamonds I mentioned earlier far surpassed
anything I had seen before. I knew all about the magnificence of
flawless blue-white stones, but up to that point I had not seen any.
But when I set eyes on them I was astounded. My idea of what they
might look like fell far short of the reality. Just so when we see Jesus
in all his glory; it will far surpass all our previous thoughts and
ideas. We shall be lost in wonder and amazement.

In the meantime we must not forget for a single moment that God has called us for this very purpose, that we should share the glory of Jesus. As Paul says to the believers in Thessalonica, God 'called you to this through our gospel, that you might share in the glory of our Lord Jesus Christ' (2 Thessalonians 2:14). The pressures and responsibilities of daily life can all too easily cause us to forget that we have an appointment with Jesus and that we are to make ourselves ready for it. We may be like a friend of mine who was going to meet his bride-to-be for an evening out and went upstairs to change his shirt. He got undressed, put on his pyjamas and got into bed! In his prayer to his Father, Jesus says: 'I want those you have given me to be with me where I am, and to see my glory, the glory you have given me because you loved me before the creation of the world' (John 17:24). How can we, who are the beneficiaries of this prayer, possibly forget? When it comes to our high calling, fixing our eyes on Jesus is the only cure for amnesia.

Promises about our glorious destiny are numerous in the New Testament. Jesus promised his disciples: 'I confer on you a kingdom, just as my Father conferred one on me, so that you may eat and drink at my table in my kingdom…' (Luke 22:29, 30). To the church in Laodicea he said: 'To him who overcomes, I will give the right to sit with me on my throne…' (Revelation 3:21). Paul adds his confirmation: It is God 'who calls you into his kingdom and glory' (1 Thessalonians 2:12). The Father has qualified us 'to share in the inheritance of the saints in the kingdom of light. For he has rescued us from the dominion of darkness and brought us into the kingdom of the Son he loves…' (Colossians 1:12-13).

Driving along the motorway in the summer, I was overtaken by another car. The driver was fairly elderly, as was the lady sitting next to him. A suitcase was strapped to the roof rack. A sticker in the rear window read: 'We are spending our kids' inheritance.' Obviously the notice was not intended to be taken seriously, but it did raise a question in my mind. Why should their children expect an inheritance? What had they done to deserve it? After all, the

parents had probably spent a fortune on the upbringing and education of their children and had no doubt worked very hard to build up
their capital for their retirement. Why shouldn't they spend it?

But we all know it does not work like that. Most responsible
parents would want to make sure, if at all possible, that they leave
their children comfortably off. Their only qualification to be named
in the will however, is their status as sons and daughters. So it is
with us. We qualify to share in the glory of Christ because God has
adopted us as his children. The Judge of the world is now our
Father, and we have done nothing to deserve it. Hear the rapturous
words of the apostle: 'For you did not receive a spirit that makes
you a slave again to fear, but you received the Spirit of sonship. And
by him we cry "*Abba,* Father." The Spirit himself testifies with our
spirit that we are God's children. Now if we are children, then we
are heirs – heirs of God and co-heirs with Christ...' (Romans 8:15-17).

The same principle applied in the distribution of the land of
Canaan to the children of Israel. None of them deserved an inheritance in the promised land and yet, because they were privileged to
be sons of Israel and the offspring of Abraham, they received the
portion of land that was allotted to them. We too have a portion of
the heavenly Canaan reserved for us; as sons of the Most High we
too 'will receive the kingdom and will possess it for ever – yes, for
ever and ever' (Daniel 7:18).

The temporary nature of the inheritance in Canaan made it
impossible for the hope of Abraham to be realised on this earth, and
he knew it. So, the temporary nature of this world makes it impossible for our hope to be realised here. Faith cannot give way to sight
as long as we are in this body, and for the same reason our hope
cannot yet be realised. Like Abraham, we are 'looking forward to
the city with foundations, whose architect and builder is God'
(Hebrews 11:10).

3. Rejoicing in Hope

Some years ago I was on holiday in the Lake District with my wife and family. One day, quite unexpectedly, we bumped into an acquaintance of mine who had just been water skiing on Lake Windermere. To the delight of my children, he offered to teach them how to ski and arranged to meet us the following day. The children's hopes were so high that my wife and I did not have the heart to tell them we were not convinced our 'friend' would keep his word. Imagine their bitter disappointment when he did not turn up!

Experiences like this are not uncommon in this life and as we grow older we learn not to get too excited about hopes that are easily frustrated. How different it is with our hope of glory. Nothing else in this life provides such a solid foundation for rejoicing, and for this reason, our rejoicing is elevated far above the joys of this world. If we have the assurance that we are among that number given to Jesus by his Father – those for whom he prayed, that they would see his glory – what more can we want? His prayer cannot possibly fail in its object, and for this reason our rejoicing is *never* inappropriate.

Without this assurance we shall not be able to rejoice when things appear to go wrong. How, for example, can we rejoice when we are insulted, persecuted, or falsely accused, unless we know that our reward in heaven is great? (Matthew 5:11, 12). How can we rejoice in our sufferings if we are not persuaded that God is using them to mould our character and strengthen our hope in preparation for that great day? 'We... rejoice in our sufferings' says Paul, 'because we know that suffering produces perseverance; perseverance character; and character hope' (Romans 5:3, 4). The apostle does not mean to imply that we *enjoy* our sufferings; in that case they would not be sufferings at all. We cannot rejoice *because* of them, but we can rejoice *in* them, for we no longer see them as meaningless, or as expressions of God's displeasure, but as tokens of his love, always providing we are not wilfully clinging to some cherished sin, but even then the chastisement is still a token of his love. We rejoice because we know that we belong to that privileged number who are 'the objects of his mercy, whom he prepared in advance for glory – even us, whom he also called, not only from the Jews but also from the Gentiles' (Romans 9:23, 24). To say the least, it would be inappropriate to find such privileged people miserable. We shall come back to this subject in chapter ten.

4. The Patience of Hope

Patience is the product of hope. 'For everything that was written in the past' says Paul, 'was written to teach us, so that through endurance and the encouragement of the Scriptures we might have hope' (Romans 15:4). The patience of which Paul speaks is the steadfast endurance of suffering in all its forms. It expresses itself in patient waiting. 'Who hopes for what he already has?' asks the apostle, 'But if we hope for what we do not yet have, we wait for it patiently' (Romans 8:24, 25). The apostle also speaks of endurance as being 'inspired by hope in our Lord Jesus Christ' (1 Thessalonians 1:3). Those who do not have the hope cannot have the patience.

This patience of hope is a rare quality today. Some it seems are totally blind to the link between faith and endurance, and think of the former as conveying the right to claim deliverance from suffering here and now. That believers should suffer the disappointments and heartaches of this life is seen, not as evidence of persevering faith, but as an indication of the lack of it. Faith for them, is not a means of strength to endure, but a way of escape. Having been duped into believing that suffering serves no useful purpose, they expect to be saved from it without waiting. Why should God allow those whom he loves to suffer? Why should he allow the pain to continue a moment longer when he has given us the faith to end it?

The patience of hope however takes a much longer view – a view that is much more consistent with the teaching of the Bible. The old word 'longsuffering' preserves the true meaning of the virtue; we are content to suffer long, knowing that deliverance will come in God's time and certainly when his glory is revealed in us (Romans 8:18). Trials come, Peter says, 'so that your faith – of greater worth than gold, which perishes even though refined by fire – may be proved genuine and may result in praise, glory and honour when Jesus Christ is revealed' (1 Peter 1:7). How much can God refine our faith through suffering if, by so doing, he gives us more power to endure it! One evidence of true faith will be seen in the fact that we frequently find ourselves giving thanks for all the precious lessons we have learned through our trials, even though they were hard to endure at the time. And if we would only pay more attention to Scripture we would freely acknowledge that it is impossible to believe its teaching and still cling to the idea that faith is the key to a trouble-free life.

If, on the other hand, we are impatient and start asking foolish questions like, 'what have I done to deserve this?' the lessons will be missed, and we shall know nothing of the benefits of sharing in Christ's sufferings (Romans 8:17). 'In this world you will have trouble' Jesus said, 'But take heart! I have overcome the world' (John 16:33). 'Anyone who does not take his cross and follow me is not worthy of me' (Matthew 10:38). So let us settle it in our minds that faith does not provide a way of escape from suffering, whether it be pain or persecution. All who live godly lives will suffer persecution and whatever the form it takes, we must be willing to be martyrs. Our duty is to strive to 'imitate those who through faith and patience inherit what has been promised' (Hebrews 6:12).

5. The Encouragement of Hope

In a recent court case a high profile politician was charged with lying under oath. This offence is considered to be a more serious matter than just lying, although it is not easy to say why. The commandment simply says 'You shall not give false testimony against your neighbour' (Exodus 20:16). If people are prepared to lie when they are not under oath, what makes us think they will not do so when they are? I remember feeling some resentment when I was handed a Bible in court and asked to swear that I would tell the truth, the whole truth and nothing but the truth. I felt like saying to the attendant, 'excuse me, there's no need for that, I'm not in the habit of telling lies.' (There is some evidence however that God sees some forms of lying to be more serious than others. Compare Joshua 2:4-6 with Acts 5:1-11).

Would it not then be superfluous – even an insult – to ask God, who cannot lie, to take an oath to confirm his word? What would our friends think if we refused to accept their word unless they were prepared to swear on oath? Would they not be deeply offended? What a surprise it is then, to discover that in consideration of our weakness, God *has* confirmed his word with an oath: 'When God made his promise to Abraham, since there was no one greater for him to swear by, he swore by himself, saying, "I will surely bless you and give you many descendants." And so after waiting patiently, Abraham received what was promised. Men swear by someone greater than themselves, and the oath confirms what is said and puts an end to all argument. Because God wanted to make the unchanging nature of his purpose very clear to the heirs of what was promised, he confirmed it with an oath. God did this so that, by two unchangeable things in which it is impossible for God to lie, we who have fled to take hold of the hope offered to us may be greatly encouraged' (Hebrews 6:13-18).

To benefit from the encouragement provided by these 'two unchangeable things', we need to go back to Genesis. We need to understand that all who are born of the Spirit, are born into a church with a history going back, not merely to New Testament times, but to the time of Abraham who lived about four thousand years ago. Although in Old Testament times Abraham's natural descendants were regarded as his children, we learn from the New Testament that they are now his spiritual descendants, in the sense that they have the same faith as he. As Paul teaches: 'If you belong to Christ, then you are Abraham's seed, and heirs according to the promise' (Galatians 3:29). Under the terms of the covenant of grace, the blessings promised to Abraham are also promised to us – and confirmed with an oath (Genesis 22:15-18)!

It was therefore for *our* encouragement that the promise and the oath were made. And how do we inherit the promise? By faith, just as Abraham did. As Paul says: 'It was not through law that Abraham and his offspring received the promise that he would he heir of the world, but through the righteousness that comes by faith... Therefore, the promise comes by faith, so that it may be by grace and may be guaranteed to all Abraham's offspring – not only to those who are of the law, but also to those who are of the faith Abraham. He is the father of us all' (Romans 4:13, 16). Paul is saying that the only way to inherit the promises (whether by Jew or Gentile) is by grace through faith in Christ. We then are the ones who are to be heirs of the world, along with everyone who is saved by grace through faith. What greater encouragement can we have?

6. What Are We Hoping For?

A lot has been said about the nature of our hope, and the dramatic effect it has on our lives here and now, but what is it we are hoping for, and when will our hope be realised? It is often assumed that since our future glory is of a totally different dimension from anything we experience in this world, the finite human mind cannot possibly cope with it. For God to try and reveal it to us would be rather like describing the colours of the rainbow to a blind man. This is a serious mistake. It is true, of course, that there are many aspects of the glory to come that we cannot understand, but we are certainly not left in total ignorance about it. Scripture provides many thrilling insights as to the nature of our glorification, and although we always run out of adjectives in trying to describe it, it is both legitimate and stimulating to do so.

Of all the words of the marriage service vows, 'till death us do part,' are probably the most well-known. They are a solemn reminder that death separates us from one another. It separates husbands from wives, parents from children, and it brings friendships to an abrupt end. Sooner or later, each one of us will be called to go through that dark valley alone. In sharp contrast, our glorification will be the biggest and happiest reunion the world has ever seen. 'For the Lord himself will come down from heaven, with a loud command, with the voice of the archangel and with the trumpet of God, and the dead in Christ will rise first. After that, we who are still alive and are left will be caught up with them in the clouds to meet the Lord in the air. And so we will be with the Lord forever' (1 Thessalonians 4:16, 17). In these words, the apostle Paul makes it very clear that all believers – those who are living and those who have died – will all be gathered together with the Lord Jesus Christ in glory.

It is obvious then, that glorification does not take place when a believer dies. At death, believers are immediately and consciously 'at home with the Lord' (2 Corinthians 5:8). Death for the believer will bring him into the presence and perfect likeness of the Lord he loves. It will set him free from temptation, from the constraints of his ignorance, and from everything that now mars his joy in Christ. In comparison with this life, with its trials and temptations, its griefs and disappointments, to be with Christ is 'better by far' (Philippians 1:23). But this is not glorification.

Christians who think of material things as essentially evil are at a disadvantage here. They think of this physical earth as evil and therefore destined for total destruction; and of heaven as a perfect but insubstantial place, where the blissful souls of the faithful departed float about in space! If it is so good to be with Christ, they say, what more do we need? But God has not given up on his earth, no matter how much it has been spoiled by the people who have lived in it; nor has he given up on our physical bodies even though, on account of sin, they have returned to dust. When the Lord Jesus returns, not only shall we have brand new bodies like the glorious body of Christ (Philippians 3:21), but also a re-created universe in which to live. In that new world, there will be no tears, no ageing, no pain, because death will have been be abolished (Revelation 21:1-4). The new heaven and new earth will be our home - 'the home of righteousness' (2 Peter 3:13).

We see then, that the glorification of the believer does not co-incide with death, but with the destruction of death. Death was introduced because of sin, and as far as believers are concerned, it should hold no terrors. Even so, it is still a formidable foe. Because of it, we lose our friends, our health, and our faculties, and eventually our lives. Death is the 'last enemy,' yet to be destroyed by Christ (1 Corinthians 15:26). But in the coming glorious moment when the saints are glorified, death will be a thing of the past. This is the event for which we long. For even we, says Paul, 'who have the firstfruits of the Spirit, groan inwardly as we wait eagerly for our adoption as sons, the redemption of our bodies. For in this hope we were saved' (Romans 8:23). And if the universe could talk, what would it say? According to Paul, it would say: 'I too am groaning, like a woman in the pains of childbirth, waiting to be liberated from my bondage to decay, and obtain the freedom of the glory of the children of God' (Romans 8:18-23).

How then shall we describe glorification? What words shall we use to summarise it? It is a future event in which God's eternal purposes in the redemption of his people and the re-creation of his universe will be finally accomplished. Sin and death will be banished forever. All who belong to Christ – and here is where we run out of adjectives – will live perfect lives, in perfect bodies, in a perfect world, in perfect fellowship with each other and with our perfect Saviour. We shall glorify him forever, and our joy will be complete.

---

1. Moulton & Milligan *The Vocabulary of the Greek New Testament*, p660,
   Eerdmans, reprint 1980

CHAPTER EIGHT

Growing Into His Likeness

1. Maturity, the Process
2. Sanctification, the Preparation
3. Christ, the Pattern
4. Election, the Pledge
5. The Spirit, the Provider

'And we, who with unveiled faces all reflect the Lord's glory, are being transformed into his likeness with ever-increasing glory, which comes from the Lord, who is the Spirit'
(2 Corinthians 3:18).

1. Maturity, the Process

Some years ago my wife and I went to an inter-church meeting which had been called in preparation for a joint mission in the town. To our surprise, not many young people were present. The opening remarks of the speaker revealed that he too had noticed this. Looking around the room, he said: 'I see you are all mature Christians.' Then, after a brief pause, presumably to allow us to feel good, he added; 'like ripe cheese, beginning to go off!'

That 'mature' Christians do sometimes 'go off' is a sad but indisputable fact. They give the impression there is nothing else for them to learn. I have known a goodly number of these 'mature' people who gave up going to church altogether because they 'got nothing from it', or because 'things are not the same as they used to be'. But this is Christian elitism, not Christian maturity. Certainly the apostle Paul does not use the word 'mature' (Greek: teleios) to describe believers who have forsaken their first love (Revelation 4), but rather of those who are grown-up in their faith. Maturity is never a dead end. The use of the word 'perfect' (to translate teleios) in the King James Version does not help because Paul is not thinking of believers with no flaws, but of those with 'the full riches of complete understanding' (Colossians 2:2).

In the second chapter of his first letter to the Corinthians, Paul stresses his determination not to use 'wise and persuasive words' in the preaching of the gospel. But he goes on to say: 'We do however, speak a message of wisdom among the mature...' (1 Corinthians 2:6). The apostle is referring to those who are well instructed in the faith and can therefore cope with the 'solid food' of the word of God (1 Corinthians 3:2). The same word (teleios) occurs in 1 Corinthians 14:20 where the apostle tells us to 'stop thinking like children. In regard to evil be infants, but in your thinking be adults', or 'in your thinking be mature.' The word goes right to the heart of our current problem in the church, for is it not a fact that many Christians are content to be infants in their thinking? If not, why do they shy away from the serious study and exposition of the word of God, preferring what is superficial and entertaining?

A week or two ago I was in a lift with a young mother and her newly born wide-eyed baby in a pram, and three older women. All the way to the top floor of the building the baby was the centre of attraction, the three older women being almost ecstatic: 'What a beautiful baby!' 'Isn't he gorgeous?' 'What lovely eyes he's got!' I began to wonder what they would say if they, knowingly, saw the same baby, at the same apparent age, in the same pram two or three years from now. Expressions of sympathy and concern rather than gasps of admiration would then be more appropriate.

The spiritual health of those who are babes in Christ is seen in their growth towards maturity, and this is what gives such joy to those of us who are older in the faith. It is cause for great sadness when we see people who have made professions of faith but not much progress. I have no wish to be unduly pessimistic, but we cannot deny that an inordinate number of born-again believers are still in their prams when they are three or four years old, and sometimes much more. So much so, we begin to wonder whether there is any new life in them at all. The apostle Paul complained about a similar situation among the believers in Corinth. They too were very proud of their 'superior' wisdom, but in fact didn't have very much: 'Brothers, I could not address you as spiritual but as worldly – mere infants in Christ. I gave you milk, not solid food, for you were not yet ready for it. Indeed, you are still not ready. You are still worldly' (1 Corinthians 3:1-3). Paul here puts his finger on the problem. They had not grown in stature because they had not grown in knowledge; they had not progressed beyond the first principles, and it was their own fault. When believers fail to make progress towards Christian maturity, this is always where the fault lies. In other words, the evidence of growth is seen in our hunger to learn more, not because we like our intellects stretched (although that is not a bad thing) but so that our hope will be strengthened, and that we may live to please the Lord. Conversely, when believers have no appetite for the spiritual food of God's word, a serious spiritual malady is present that needs to be diagnosed and remedied as soon as possible. Christians who are not concerned about their lack of growth will probably not be reading this, but if they are, they should realise that growing to maturity is not the privilege of a favoured few, but the duty of all who believe.

To be frank, I am seldom thrilled by the sight of new-born babies. More often than not, they are a bit wizened, and it is hard to know whether they are smiling or whether it's just wind! Most female readers will strongly disagree with this observation, but I think we would all agree that babies are much more attractive at six months old, when they have put some weight on and their smile is unmistakable. Be that as it may, it is certainly true that there is more joy in seeing one Christian grow in grace (2 Peter 3:18), than in a thousand claims to a new birth that cannot be verified because growth is not evident. The apostle John puts it like this: 'I have no greater joy than to hear that my children are walking in the truth' (3 John 4).

The answer to the question then, as to why some believers grow up fast while others remain in the kindergarten, lies in the difference between their degree of devotion to the means of grace; especially the apostle's teaching (Acts 2:42). As far as they are able, believers who are eager to grow will not allow anything to divert them from worship, fellowship, teaching and prayer, and as a result they find the contemplation of Christ's glory an ever-increasing delight. Others have either never succeeded in establishing a pattern of discipline, or if they have, it has been abandoned because the affairs of this world have been allowed to take priority.

Some, through no fault of their own, are handicapped by being separated from fellowship and teaching, but even in these circumstances, with the Lord's help, the loss can be made good. Soon after his conversion, Paul went to Arabia for a time (Galatians 1:16-18) and all the evidence suggests that although he did not have access to fellowship and worship, he used the time very profitably.

Those who feel their growth has been halted by yielding to temptation should remember that the LORD upholds all those who fall (Psalm 145:14). If we confess our sins, God is always faithful to his promise to forgive us, and to purify us from all unrighteousness (1 John 1:9). We must never despair of forgiveness. And God can even use our moral lapses to further his purpose in us. I have known believers to make good progress after a grievous and lengthy lapse of some kind, so eager were they to learn from their mistake and to make good 'the years the locusts have eaten' (Joel 2:25).

Those who really want to grow, but grieve over their inability to understand, should not feel discouraged. Paradoxically, believers who are dissatisfied with their progress are usually making more than they think, and certainly much more than those who are content with it. To be discontented with our spiritual development is usually a sign of spiritual health. To be content with it is a disease.

I remember a woman in her middle fifties who mourned over her slowness to learn; a state of mind that could not have existed had she not been so eager. Only illness and emergencies would keep her away from the weekly Bible-study and prayer meeting and she always listened intently. Her frequent complaint at the end of the meeting was, 'I didn't understand half of it.' On one occasion when she was particularly troubled about not having understood 'half of it', I ventured to suggest that I found her complaint encouraging, because if she had not understood 'half of it,' presumably she had understood the other half. It soon became obvious to everyone except herself that this was indeed the case. She was learning fast, and yet she never stopped complaining!

2. Sanctification, the Preparation

The word 'sanctified' has two meanings: to set apart for sacred use and to be made holy. Believers are set apart for God from the moment of our spiritual birth. But we are also being made holy in preparation for the glory to come. Sanctification in the latter sense is a very practical thing. 'For the grace of God that brings salvation has appeared to all men' says Paul to Titus. 'It teaches us to say "No" to ungodliness and worldly passions, and to live self-controlled, upright and godly lives in this present age, while we wait for the blessed hope – the glorious appearing of our great God and Saviour, Jesus Christ…' (Titus 2:11-13). Every cause has an effect, and in these verses Paul explains that the grace of God is the cause, and sanctification the effect. Negatively, the effect is saying 'No' to ungodliness and worldly passions. Positively, it is living self-controlled, upright and godly lives. Both the negative and positive side of our sanctification are necessary as we wait for the appearing of our Saviour. In the present social climate, the negative side needs to be stressed, especially to young (in age) believers who are under great pressure to conform 'to the pattern of this world' (Romans 12:2), and for whom saying 'no' can be costly.

Just as a dead-line is imposed on athletes who prepare for the race, or students who study for an examination, so a dead-line is imposed on Christians who prepare to meet their Lord. The only difference is that we do not know the precise time of our dead-line, because the time of our death, or the time of the Lord's return, whichever comes first, is unknown. But our time is limited nevertheless, and we should never rest on our laurels. Our schooling for glory may end sooner than we think.

One of my hobbies is landscape painting. These days I never attempt to paint a picture from memory, because every time I try I always make a mess of it, in spite of the fact that I viewed the scene until I felt sure I had committed it to memory. Therefore, to paint a good picture I need to have the subject before my eyes all the time. Not all artists would agree with this. They would insist that the picture must express personality. But I prefer to paint exactly what I see, not least because I always find God's creation more attractive than what comes out of my head! I do not object to the idea of expressing personality through painting even though I am not good at it, but when it comes to imitating the life of Christ, it is no use trying to work from memory, and to rely on the imagination is disastrous. I need to fix my eyes on Jesus all the time. As for my personality, it is my failure to look to Jesus that hinders me from being the person God wants me to be, because I soon forget what excellence I have seen in Jesus.

As we have seen so many times before in these pages, 'whenever anyone turns to the Lord, the veil is taken away' so that we are able, by faith, to see the glory of the Lord and be transformed into his likeness (2 Corinthians 3:16-18). As the context shows, Paul is talking about Moses, whose face was so radiant after he had been speaking with the Lord, the people were afraid to come near him. It was necessary therefore to put a veil over his face until the glory faded. (Exodus 34:29-35). Paul's point is that the veil is still there, but now it is over the hearts of unbelievers, so that they are unable to see the glory of Christ. But for believers, the veil has been removed so that we may see Jesus and be transformed into his likeness with ever increasing glory. The New International Version gives an alternative reading: 'And we, who with unveiled faces contemplate the Lord's glory…' This is probably better because the veil has been removed, not so that we may have a fleeting glimpse of the beauty and excellence of Christ, but may contemplate his glory and by degrees be changed into his likeness. To condense this into a simple and easily memorised principle, we may say, 'regular contemplation of the beauty of Jesus is essential to our growth in holiness.'

It is said that people who live with each other for a long time, grow to be like each other in their mannerisms, and sometimes even in their appearance. I have even heard it said that dogs grow to be like their masters. Whether it is true or not is a matter of opinion, but it is certainly true that those who live with Christ day by day, grow to be like him. And when does the process begin? As soon as our eyes are opened to his glory!

Our view of him by faith will never be perfect, nor indeed our transformation into his likeness, but the process must begin here and now because it is a necessary preparation for the day when we shall see him in all his beauty and perfection (1 John 3:2). To entertain the hope of glory without making any preparation for it is the fantasy of unbelievers.

In an informal Bible-study group I tried to use marriage as an illustration of this process. 'It's like being married,' I said, 'if husband and wife know each other in a loving relationship, they not only understand each other more and more, but grow to be like each other. So it is with our relationship with the Lord Jesus Christ. Once united with him, we begin to know him better day by day and grow to be like him…' At this point an elderly lady interrupted. 'No, no' she said, 'I've lived with Tom for fifty years and I still don't know him.' The interruption caused some amusement and probably exposed the limitations of my illustration, but everyone in the room knew that Tom and his wife had a very stable and loving relationship. Not only that, they had grown like each other much more that she was prepared to admit.

A moment ago I said that entertaining the hope of glory without making any preparation for it is the fantasy of unbelievers. Seldom is this more obvious than at funerals of the godless. Joining in conversation with the mourners often provides an insight into the way they think. Many seem to feel it is their duty to tell the close relatives of the deceased not to worry because he or she has gone to a better place. I have known people to give such empty assurances in spite of the fact that everyone present knew the deceased was grossly immoral. What folly to think we can live thoroughly godless lives and expect to enter into the presence of Christ when we die! Death is gain only for those who live for Christ (Philippians 1:21). If we see no glory in Jesus in this life, we have no grounds for hoping to be with him in the next.

The very few people who are converted to Christ when they are dying may be thought of as exceptions to this rule, but even they see something of his glory. Otherwise they would not have turned to Christ. The Gospel record shows that the dying thief who, in the throes of death, turned to the Lord and said: 'Jesus, remember me when you come into your kingdom,' saw something wonderful in Jesus that his fellow malefactor could not see. Jesus answered: 'I tell you the truth, today you will be with me in paradise' (Luke 23:42, 43).

But we who, in the mercy of God, have been given time to grow, should not be so ignorant as to think that sanctification is not a mandatory preparation for the completion of our salvation. There is no ambiguity in Scripture: 'Without holiness no one will see the Lord' (Hebrews 12:14). The words of Paul too, make it very clear that believers are chosen in order to be holy. Again and again he stresses the point: God predestined us 'to be conformed to the likeness of his Son' (Romans 8:29); we are 'called to be saints' (Romans 1:7), which means we are called to 'live a life worthy of the calling' we have received (Ephesians 4:1). 'But we ought always to thank God for you, brothers loved by the Lord,' says Paul, 'because from the beginning God chose you to be saved through the sanctifying work of the Spirit and through belief in the truth. He called you to this through our gospel, that you might share in the glory of our Lord Jesus Christ' (2 Thessalonians 2:13, 14). The purpose of our election is not salvation and holiness, as if the two could exist separately, but salvation through holiness. We are saved by faith alone, but faith that does not lead to sanctification is dead.

Paul made the same point in his farewell address to the Ephesian elders: 'Now I commit you to God and to the word of his grace, which can build you up and give you an inheritance among all those who are sanctified' (Acts 20:32). The implication is plain; if we are to receive the inheritance among those who are sanctified, we too must be sanctified. 'Both the one who makes men holy and those who are made holy are of the same family. So Jesus is not ashamed to call them brothers' (Hebrews 2:11). Although Jesus is the Son of God in his own right and we are sons by adoption, we are nevertheless members of the same family. And what binds the family together? The bond of holiness! Therefore, if we are privileged to be called brothers of the Lord Jesus, we have a solemn duty to ensure that there is nothing in our lives of which he, our brother, would be ashamed. The family likeness must be evident.

3. Christ, the Pattern

The word 'pattern' comes from the Latin word *pater* meaning father. The idea is that just as a father sets an example (or should do so), so a pattern is something to be followed. In this sense, Jesus is our pattern because he shows us exactly what our heavenly Father is like. Our duty is to follow him closely. John puts it concisely: 'Whoever claims to live in him must walk as Jesus did' (1 John 2:6).

To follow the example of Jesus has to do with our attitude as well as our actions; for if our actions are to be right, then so must our attitude be. The importance of this was stressed by Paul in his letter to the Philippians: 'Your attitude should be the same as that of Christ Jesus.' And what was his attitude? Being in very nature God, he 'did not consider equality with God something to be grasped, but made himself nothing' (Philippians 2:5-7). His actions were right because his attitude was right. Take for example his life of prayer.

Although he was very busy (Mark 3:20) he always found time for prayer (Matthew 14:23) because this was the tenor of his life. His petitions and intercessions expressed his lifelong submission to his Father's will. We shall never attain the same degree of humility as Jesus, but his attitude must always be our pattern.

The feet of Jesus were always firmly on the ground however. He could not be accused of being detached from the real world. Tragically, we cannot deny that when some believers are accused of having their heads in the clouds, the charge is often just. But we are called to be heavenly-minded, not absent-minded. Our minds are to be 'set on what the Spirit desires' (Romans 8:5) so that we may live lives of practical holiness in this world. This is the spiritual principle by which we live and grow. Absent-mindedness on the other hand, is the lack of mental discipline to apply our minds to the job in hand.

My wife and I were invited out for dinner. Some time before the meal was served our hostess asked her husband to fetch a pan from the scullery. But five minutes later he had not returned and his wife went to see what had happened to him. She found him in the study reading a book. Glancing in our direction with a roll of the eyeballs and a disapproving shake of the head she said, 'his mind is always on something else.' The husband's absent-mindedness did nothing to improve the marriage, which later ended in divorce.

It is in this area of human relationships that our conformity to Christ will be tested most severely – especially in the church. It is not possible to be involved in the life of the church for long without discovering that some Christians can be difficult, sometimes very difficult, (and sometimes even the 'mature' ones). The capacity of some believers to harbour grievances, sometimes for years on end, is lamentable. Others do not know how to react graciously when criticised and find it very hard to admit they are wrong, even when they know it. They stand on their pride and make it very clear how deeply hurt they are. They go out of their way to avoid the 'offender', and never think of adopting the role of peacemaker. Yet others are quick to lose their temper and use bitter words, and never stop to think they are grieving the Spirit. In this situation, in the home and in the world, we are called to be like Jesus, whose attitude was very different: 'When they hurled insults at him, he did not retaliate; when he suffered, he made no threats. Instead, he entrusted himself to him who judges justly' (1 Peter 2:23).

At the time of my conversion, it was quite common to hear believers praying earnestly for the beauty of Jesus to be seen in their lives. Today, such prayers are seldom heard. The very thought of holiness as being the beauty of Jesus shining through us is rare. But this is the essence of it. It is also the essence of fellowship, for 'if we walk in the light as he is in the light, we have fellowship with one another' (1 John 1:7). Take careful note of the Lord's words in his prayer to his Father: 'I have given them the glory that you gave me, that they may be one as we are one: I in them and you in me. May they be brought to complete unity to let the world know that you sent me and have loved them even as you loved me' (John 17:22, 23). Many suggestions have been made as to the precise meaning of these words, but surely what Jesus is saying is that just as the Father's glory is revealed through the Son, so the glory of the Son is revealed through his disciples, and that the purpose of this revelation is to bind all believers into one family. Only by this means will unbelievers be convinced that the Father sent Jesus into the world and that our unity is the consequence of the Father's love. Of course, this unity has nothing to do with belonging to the same organisation. It is a unity between all God's holy people – those who are partakers of the glory of Christ. Since we are 'all one in Christ Jesus' (Galatians 3:28), we are under obligation to 'make every effort to keep the unity of the Spirit through the bond of peace' (Ephesians 4:3), and if Christ is our pattern we shall not fail in our duty. To do otherwise is to bring dishonour on his name.

In one church of which I was minister, two Christian women – I will call them Jane and Sandra – could not get along with each other. The breakdown in relationships went on for so long I felt it my duty to talk to them. During the interview with Jane, she said to me: 'Don't worry, things may not be right between me and Sandra, but they are right between me and the Lord.' 'What nonsense!' I replied, 'if things are not right between you and Sandra, how can they be right between you and the Lord?'

4. Election, the Pledge

It is doubtful whether there can be a more powerful incentive to holiness, a stronger deterrent against sin, and a firmer support in temptation, than the assurance that God has predestined us to be like Christ. Great will be our fear of grieving the Holy Spirit (Ephesians 4:30) if we know beyond reasonable doubt that we were chosen in Christ 'before the creation of the world' (Ephesians 1:4) to be to the praise of his glory (Ephesians 1:12). In these circumstances we shall not find it easy to grieve the God we love. As John says: 'everyone who has this hope in him purifies himself, just as he is pure' (1 John 3:3). When we fail, our grief will be all the greater, but it will be a sure sign of a heavenly frame of mind. By contrast, those who are not overwhelmed by the privilege of being God's chosen cannot feel the same hatred towards sin. This is also true the other way round. It would be easier for pigs to fly than for a Christian to love his sins and have the assurance that he has been chosen of God. Where there is no eagerness for holiness, there can be no assurance of heaven.

5. The Spirit, the Provider

Christians today would give a wide variety of answers to the question: *What is the evidence of the work of the Holy Spirit in our lives?* If the question were put to many people I have known, they would, without hesitation, mention things like speaking in tongues, receiving a word of knowledge, a revelation, a prophecy, or having the ability to work miracles, and so forth. How easily we forget that these gifts were very much in evidence in the church in Corinth and yet Paul, although not disapproving of the gifts themselves, complained about their worldliness and lack spiritual depth (1 Corinthians 3:1). Jesus too warned us that on the day of judgment there will be people who will say to him: "'Lord, Lord, did we not prophesy in your name, and in your name cast out demons and perform many miracles?" And he will say to them: "I never knew you. Away from me, you evildoers!"' (Matthew 7:22-23). As if that were not enough, Paul adds his warning: 'The coming of the lawless one will be in accordance with the work of Satan displayed in all kinds of counterfeit miracles, signs and wonders, and in every sort of evil that deceives those who are perishing' (2 Thessalonians 2:9, 10). The apostle is not saying that the Antichrist will only pretend to perform miracles. On the contrary, his miracles will be so convincing that many will be deceived.

What then is the undeniable evidence of the Spirit's work in our lives? First of all, it will be seen in our grief over past sins and our willing acknowledgement that forgiveness comes through Christ alone. (The ability to repent and believe is conveyed to us by the Spirit, Acts 5:31; 11:18). Second, we shall see more and more of the glory of Christ in the Scriptures, because it is the work of the Spirit to reveal him in this way (Hebrews 1:1-3). By contrast, 'the man without the Spirit does not accept the things that come from the Spirit of God, for they are foolishness to him and he cannot understand them, because they are spiritually discerned' (1 Corinthians 2:14). Third, we shall have an assurance in our hearts that we are the children of God because the Holy Spirit is 'the Spirit of sonship' and he 'testifies with our spirit that we are God's children' (Romans 8:15, 16). Such assurance cannot possibly originate in us. This inner consciousness that we are the objects of God's love will increase as we grow in grace and knowledge. Fourth, the fruit of the Spirit – 'love, joy, peace, patience, kindness, goodness, faithfulness, gentleness and self control' (Galatians 5:22, 23) – will be evidcnt in our lives. Fifth, we shall have the assurance that although we do not know what we ought to pray – for ourselves as well as others – the Spirit helps us in our weakness and intercedes for us (Romans 8:26).

None of this must be taken to imply that the believer is passive – like a limp balloon waiting to be filled with gas. The presence of the Spirit will never allow us to be content with inactivity (Hebrews 6:12). As Paul puts it, we shall press on towards the goal to win the prize for which God has called us heavenwards in Christ Jesus (Philippians 3:14). We are to 'make every effort to live in peace with all men and to be holy…' (Hebrews 12:14).

A coastal path runs north for many miles from my home and I have been in the habit of walking this path almost daily for many years. Frequently, I am passed by joggers who are so breathless they can hardly say 'good morning'. Even on the coldest day they pass me with perspiration pouring down their faces and dripping from the end of their noses. The effort they make and the discomfort they endure is most impressive. And all just to keep physically fit.

The strenuous preparation athletes make is even more impressive. They work hard at their daily training and adopt a strict diet. Their entire lifestyle is geared up to one thing – the winning of a medal, the glory of which will soon fade away. 'Everyone who competes in the games' says the apostle Paul, 'goes into strict training. They do it to get a crown that will not last…' If people will submit to such severe discipline to gain fleeting glory, should not we do as much 'to get a crown that will last forever' (1 Corinthians 9:25)? The athlete knows only too well that the more effort he puts into his training, the more his confidence of winning the prize will increase. So it is with every believer. Although our confidence is the gift of God, it is related to the time and effort we put into our spiritual exercises.

'Since, then, you have been raised with Christ,' says Paul, 'set your hearts on things above, where Christ is seated at the right hand of God. Set your minds on things above, not on earthly things'

(Colossians 3:1, 2). To train our minds to turn heavenwards is the duty of every believer. In time we shall find that just as the needle on a compass is drawn to magnetic north, so our hearts will be drawn to the contemplation of the glory of Christ. Our adversary will do everything he can to blur our vision and so retard our progress Our sinful nature too, will resist every effort we make because it is in conflict with the Spirit (Galatians 5:16-18). We all know how bitter this conflict can be at times, but be of good cheer – victory is certain.

'Beyond all question, the mystery of godliness is great:

> He appeared in a body,
> was vindicated by the Spirit,
> was seen by angels,
> was preached among the nations,
> was believed on in the world,
> was taken up in glory'
> *(1 Timothy 3:16).*

CHAPTER NINE

Seeing Jesus in His Word

1. The Authority of the Word
2. Reading the Word
3. Understanding the Word
   a) Try to get into the mind of the writer
   b) Compare Scripture with Scripture.
   c) Do not base teaching on narrative
   d) Beware of untrue statements
   e) Do not take everything literally
   f) Remember the Bible contains every
      thing necessary to salvation
4. Praying the Word

'These are the Scriptures that testify about me'
(John 5:39).

1. The Authority of the Word

The story is told of a minister who visited a sick woman who had been a member of his church for many years. After some conversation, she suggested they should read the Bible and pray together. Having no Bible with him, the minister asked the lady if he might borrow hers. 'Yes, of course' she replied, 'it's over there, on the table.' Picking up the front and back cover of an old Bible with just a few pages in between, most with pieces cut out, the minister said: 'But this is not a Bible; there are only a few slips of paper in it.' 'That's my Bible' the woman insisted, 'every time you told us which parts of it were not true or could not be relied on, I cut them out. That's all I have left.'

No doubt the story is fictional, but it illustrates the damage many faithless ministers do by their unbelief. Such blind leaders of the blind arrogantly think themselves capable of passing judgment on the word of God, but sooner or later they fall into a pit, together with all who are foolish enough to follow them (Matthew 15:14).

The attitude of Jesus and the apostles was very different. The authority of the Scriptures (in their case, the Old Testament) was never questioned. Jesus said: 'The Scripture cannot be broken' (John 10:35), and 'It is easier for heaven and earth to disappear than for the least stroke of a pen to drop out of the Law' (Luke 16:17). He quoted the Scriptures to settle controversies (Mark 12:24; Matthew 19:1-9), to prove his own identity and ministry (Luke 4:16-21), and as a weapon against Satan (Matthew 4:4-10). The words of Psalm 22:1 were on his lips as he hung on the cross and breathed his last: 'My God, my God, why have you forsaken me?' (Mark 15:34). What further evidence do we need to prove that for the Lord Jesus Christ the authority of the Scriptures was final, and that he made himself familiar with them?. The apostles too regarded Scripture as divinely inspired. Paul did not hesitate to say that 'All Scripture is God-breathed and is useful for teaching, rebuking, correcting and training in righteousness, so that the man of God may be thoroughly equipped for every good work' (2 Timothy 3:16-17). Peter insisted that 'no prophecy of Scripture came about by the prophet's own interpretation ... but men spoke from God as they were carried along by the Holy Spirit' (2 Peter 1:20, 21). The apostles also claimed authority for their own writings. Peter did not hesitate to say that the command of our Lord and Saviour was given through the apostles (2 Peter 3:2). John insisted that anyone who does not agree with apostolic teaching is not to be welcomed into the fellowship (2 John 10). Paul insists that the word of the apostles is actually the Word of God (1 Thessalonians 2:13). He even invokes a curse on all who preach a gospel other than the one he preached (Galatians 1:8).

The Bible has God's authority stamped all over it, not least because it is the supernatural revelation of truth that cannot be discovered by the human mind. He is the source of all revealed truth. The claim, made by many, that the human mind is the source of authority in matters of faith must be firmly rejected for the simple reason that human beings cannot know God unless he reveals himself. And in any case, without the help of the Spirit of God our natural minds, being darkened by sin, are incapable of comprehending divine truth even when it is written down. Once enlightened of course, our minds play an important role in the task of understanding the word, and further enlightenment comes as we study it and submit to its authority.

The claim made by the Roman Catholic Church to be the source of authority must also be rejected. The church of God is the product of the word of God, and not the other way round as Romans Catholics claim. Since the church is an assembly of people who believe God's word, how could she exist if the Scripture did not come first? The church of the Old Testament was built on the solid foundation of God's word, as is the church of the New, except that now God's fuller revelation to the apostles has been added. As God's word to Abraham brought the Old Testament church into being, so God's revelation to the apostles brought the New into being. Peter's sermon on the day of Pentecost was based on texts from the Old Testament, now seen in the light of Christ's death and resurrection, and 'about three thousand were added to their number that day' (Acts 2:41). As God's word gave rise to creation, so his word gave rise to the church, and therefore the only authority she has is the authority of Scripture.

It cannot be disputed that although we may learn a lot about God from creation (Romans 1:20), the further revelation of his character and will in Scripture is vital. Without it we would be totally ignorant of the way of salvation and of the glory to come. We would know nothing of truth and grace as it is revealed in the Person of Jesus Christ. God would be no more than a powerful and unknowable being, and we would be utterly lost.

We must remember however that the authority of the Bible relates to matters of faith. It has a lot of history in it, but it does not claim to be a textbook on history. It has a lot of poems in it, but it is not an authority on poetry. It has a lot of science in it, but it is not a science textbook. Its exclusive authority is seen in its ability to answer such questions as: 'What is God like?' 'How may he be known?' 'What should we believe?' 'How can we be saved?' 'How should we behave?' If then we are to fix our eyes on Jesus, and grow in his likeness, the Bible must be our only guide.

2. Reading the Word

My wife Sheila came across a box full of love-letters in the attic. They were written about forty-six years ago. We did not relish the thought of the letters being read by anyone after our departure, but before we destroyed them, I browsed through a few at random. Reading my own letters was a bit boring, but some of Sheila's letters were very interesting. For a moment I wondered why I had not bothered to read them for forty-six years. After all, they were letters from the lady I love. But I quickly realised that I had no need to read them, because my wife is here with me. Talking with her face to face is much better than reading old letters.

When we see Jesus face to face we shall have no further need to read the Bible. Seeing him in all his glory will be a thousand times better than the limited view we have of him by faith, through the word. In the meantime, however, reading his word is essential to the development of our love relationship with him. Our beloved Saviour is revealed in its pages, and the only way to know him better, is to know his word better.

King David was wise to the importance of reading the word. He prayed: 'Open my eyes that I may see wonderful things in your law' (Psalm 119:18). The fuller revelation of the New Testament was not available to him, and yet he regarded God's word as the only and adequate source of spiritual enlightenment. Indeed, he loved it. 'I delight in your law... The law from your mouth is more precious to me than thousands of pieces of silver and gold... Oh, how I love your law! I meditate on it all day long... How sweet are your promises to my taste, sweeter than honey to my mouth...' (Psalm 119:70, 72, 97, 103). Job was able to say: 'I have treasured the words of his mouth more than my daily bread' (Job 23:12). When we begin to treasure God's word like this, Jesus will become all the more precious to us. But if we think we know better than David and Job and innumerable others like them, we are heading for the rocks on which our faith is likely to be shipwrecked (1 Timothy 1:19). Aversion to the Scriptures is a symptom of spiritual death.

Going back to those love-letters; when I first received them, I would read them again and again, not only to make sure there was nothing I had missed, but simply because I loved reading them. Why? Because they were written by the girl I loved, and still do. It was not the quality of the paper or the ink that captivated me but the message they conveyed. That's how it was with David and Job. They loved God's word because they loved God. And should we not take even greater delight in his word, now that we have the New Testament Scriptures to bring the glory and beauty of Jesus into sharper focus?

After expressing his love for the word, King David goes on to say 'Your commands make me wiser than my enemies… I have more insight than all my teachers… I have more understanding than the elders' (Psalm 119:97-100). Paul makes the same point to young Timothy: '…from infancy you have known the holy Scriptures, which are able to make you wise for salvation through faith in Christ Jesus' (2 Timothy 3:15). As a source of wisdom, the Scriptures have no equal. They give us an insight into the mind of God that is unobtainable anywhere else. Not that such wisdom is acquired merely by knowing the word in our minds; it comes through knowing Christ the living Word who is revealed in its pages, for he 'has become for us wisdom from God' (1 Corinthians 1:30).

That so many Christians now seem to have little love for the Bible and therefore do not turn to its pages regularly and expectantly, is a loss of incalculable proportions. According to recent surveys, the majority are now in this category. Ignorance of the word has become so widespread that many people who call themselves evangelicals find it hard to say what a Christian is. My plea to these people is simple but urgent: Come back to your roots. Come back to the Bible. Stand again with Jesus and the apostles in making Scripture your final court of appeal; the authentic and sufficient revelation of God through which the Spirit still speaks today. If you no longer believe this, integrity demands that you no longer call yourselves evangelicals. In this case you must understand that a developing awareness of Christ's glory and a strengthening expectation of the glory to come is no longer open to you.

3. Understanding the Word

To benefit from our reading, we must take care to understand it correctly. One Sunday afternoon I was chatting with members of a church youth group. Still vivid in my memory is the contribution made by one of the young men present, whom I knew to be an aircraft enthusiast. In some excitement he announced to the group that helicopters are predicted in the Bible. When I asked where the prophecy might be, he turned to Ezekiel 1:24: 'When the creatures moved, I heard the sound of their wings, like the roar of rushing waters… When they stood still, they lowered their wings.'

This is a rather extreme example of how not to use the Bible. The error in this case may be called 'imposition', imposing a meaning on the text that is not there. The idea of helicopters did not originate in the text but in the mind of the reader. We may find this amusing, but it is surprising how many believers do this, even when the outcome is much more serious. Many preachers are also guilty of it. They do not take the trouble to study the context carefully and prayerfully to determine the meaning of a text, but impose on it a meaning of their own. More often than not, this is because they bring certain presuppositions to the texts that prevent them from looking at it with fresh eyes. Therefore, instead of saying what it means, they say what they would like it to mean, or what they have been told it means. This is a dangerous and divisive practice. Think, for example, of the millions who have been deceived – to say nothing of the blood that has been spilt – because a wrong meaning was imposed on just four words from the lips of Jesus. I refer to the words: 'This is my body' or 'This is my blood…' (Matthew 26:26, 28). The idea arising from this error – that the bread and wine in the communion service are changed in to Christ's own flesh and blood –

is not only reprehensible, but destroys the meaning of the words altogether. Since Jesus himself was present, how could the words mean that the bread and wine were being changed into his flesh and blood? What sense would it have made to the disciples? Jesus himself described the contents of the cup as 'this fruit of the vine' after he gave it to his disciples. Jesus also said: 'I am the door,' 'I am the vine,' but no one supposes that any change is taking place. We have an even more potentially shocking statement in John 6:53 where Jesus says to his disciples: 'I tell you the truth, unless you eat the flesh of the Son of Man and drink his blood, you have no life in you.' The disciples were perplexed and offended, not least because the idea of drinking blood was repugnant to the Jews. Jesus then provided the key to the meaning of his words: 'The Spirit gives life; the flesh counts for nothing. The words I have spoken to you are Spirit and they are life' (John 6:63).

The opposite of imposition is exposition. To expose (expound) a passage of Scripture means to lay its meaning open for all to see. It means explaining what the text really means, and not what we would like it to mean. Even if we are not preachers, we have a duty to determine the precise meaning of the text, even if we sometimes do not like what we find.

Christians who are aware of the complex science of interpretation (known as hermeneutics) but have little knowledge of it, might be tempted to despair of finding the right meaning of many texts. But we should not be alarmed. The most untutored person with the Holy Spirit living in his heart will be able to understand more of the Scriptures than the cleverest unbeliever. The Spirit is the one who sheds light on the pages of Scripture so that we are able to discover its meaning. This does not mean however, that we need not give ourselves to study. But it does mean that as we do so, we may yet discover that on some matters we are wrong. At least, we must always be open to the possibility. When it happens, we should ask God for grace to admit it.

A good teacher is of course, a great help, but alas, they are few and far between these days. We said earlier that we are more privileged than the early disciples because they could not understand much of the teaching of Jesus until after the resurrection and the outpouring of the Spirit. But with some justification we may be tempted to think that the believers in Acts chapter two who devoted themselves to the apostles' teaching sessions were better off than many of us (Acts 2:42). Even so, we should remember that the apostles' teaching is all set out for our benefit in the books and letters of the New Testament. The apostle John makes this very clear in the preface to his first letter: 'We proclaim to you what we have seen and heard, so that you also may have fellowship with us. And our fellowship is with the Father and with his Son Jesus Christ' (1 John 1:3-4). Thank God for the faithfulness of the apostles in passing on the 'Word of life' to future generations of believers, so that we, with them, may be one in fellowship with each other and with the Father and the Son. If then, we are starved of good teaching – and that must now be the majority – private study is all the more important.

The following general guidelines are intended to help those believers who want to know Christ better but have had little or no guidance in the matter of understanding the Bible. They should help in avoiding some of the more common pitfalls:

a) Try to get into the mind of the writer. Remember that the text cannot mean anything other than it was intended to mean, and therefore we must always read the context. If we try to grasp the meaning of a text in isolation, we run a high risk of misunderstanding the intention of the author, and this can lead to all sorts of trouble. Take for example, the following text which used to be a favourite to hang on the wall: 'We know that in all things God works for the good of those who love him' (Romans 8:28). As it stands, this is only a half-truth, and half-truths easily become untruths. When we put the text back into its context, we discover that the full-stop after the words 'those who love him' should be a comma. The words after the comma, 'who have been called according to his purpose', are vital to the meaning of the whole text. The first half describes the character of those for whom God works for good: they love him; the second half tells us who these people are and why he works for their good: they are called according to his purpose. God does not work for our good merely because we love him, but also because we are his elect children. In fact, if we were not his elect, we would not love him at all. In any case, if our love for him were the only condition of his favour towards us, what security would we have? What would happen when our love burns low?

The current idea that the Spirit will bring different meanings out of the same text to suit different people or different circumstances must be firmly rejected. A moment's thought will show that if any Bible text has several different meanings, then those who say 'you can make the Bible say anything you want' are right.

Reading what scholars have written on any particular passage of Scripture will be a great help. But they must be reliable scholars – those whose sincere aim is to get at the true meaning of the text.

b) Compare Scripture with Scripture. In spite of what many critics say, the Bible does not contradict itself, although in some places it may appear to do so. A good example – one that used to trouble me soon after my conversion when I did not understand the passage properly – is found in Galatians chapter six. In the second verse Paul tells us to 'Carry each other's burdens.' But in verse five we are told that 'each one should carry his own load' (King James Version: 'bear his own burden'). Careful reading of the context will show that verse two is saying that we must sympathise with others in their troubles and do what we can to help them. Verse five means we must take responsibility for our own actions.

In cases where apparent contradiction is not easy to reconcile, we must always consult other Scriptures on the same topic. The golden rule must be: Always use the clear texts to interpret the not-so-clear ones. If we assume a meaning on a single text that is contrary to many other texts that are clear, we may be sure we have got it wrong.

c) Do not base teaching on narrative. Many mistakes are made by ignoring this simple rule. We need only think of the confusion that exists over the meaning of Acts chapter two, to realise what a hazardous practice it is. Luke's account of the outpouring of the Spirit at Pentecost is purely narrative and was not intended to set a pattern for everyone.

I have known sincere believers do the most absurd things on the basis of some verses in the Gospels or the Acts of the Apostles that are simply relating events. I think of a lady who thought that the act of the prostitute in wetting the feet of Jesus with her tears and wiping them with her hair (Luke 7:38), was a pattern for all Christian women. Accordingly, she let her hair grow very long, so that if Jesus should return in her lifetime, she would be ready to wipe his feet!

d) Beware of untrue statements. At first sight, this may cause alarm to readers who are not familiar with the Bible, but we should not flinch at the idea that some untrue statements are contained within it. I am referring of course to statements that we are not intended to believe, and not to those passages rejected by critics just because they find them hard to believe. Perhaps the best example is found in the Book of Job where Job's comforters insisted that his suffering was due to his own sin. Since this was not true, we have no right to quote the words of Zophar, Eliphaz, or Bildad to prove that Job suffered because of his sins. At the end of the book we learn that God was not pleased with the would-be comforters and said to Eliphaz: 'I am angry with you and your two friends, because you have not spoken of me what is right, as my servant Job has' (Job 42:7). We can learn a lot from what Job's comforters say, but they did not speak the word of God.

e) Do not take everything literally. We might think it unnecessary to mention this, but it is surprising how many have gone astray through failing to observe it. We have already seen the damage that has been done by taking some words of Jesus literally. It should be obvious to all of us that when Jesus said things like: 'If your right eye causes you to sin, gouge it out and throw it away' (Matthew 5:29) he was not expecting to be taken literally. He was stressing the need to be drastic with sin. Similarly, when he said: 'If anyone comes to me and does not hate his father and mother, his wife and children, his brothers and sisters...he cannot be my disciple' (Luke 14:26), he was teaching that our loyalty to him must be so great that our love for others will seem like hatred in comparison. Jesus often said shocking things, and we are left to work out their meaning in the light of the rest of his teachings

f) Remember the Bible contains everything necessary to salvation. This is particularly important in the current situation because the idea that the Bible needs to be supplemented by further revelations has once again made inroads into the church. The idea of Jesus revealing God solely through the pages of Holy Writ is now seen by many as too restricting. These further revelations, so it is claimed, are received by means of prophecies, visions and impressions. Usually, the people who claim to have such revelations are not well grounded in the Scriptures and are unaware of the rich treasures they contain. If they were, the idea of extra revelations would not be so attractive. As things stand, the receiving of messages directly from heaven (as they believe) is much more exciting than the daily painstaking study of the Bible. But to try to add to the biblical revelation can only result in taking away from it.

The Bible is like a landscape painting in which the artist has taken care to ensure that the eye of the person looking at his finished work is taken into the picture to a focal point. To add to the painting would defeat the artist's intention. It would draw the attention of the viewer away from that focal point. The Bible is God's finished work and the focal point is the Lord Jesus Christ. If we are to keep our eyes on our beloved Lord, we must be diligent students of his word, and not allow anyone to persuade us that further revelations are either valid or needed. Otherwise our view of Jesus will be distorted.

It is also now quite common for believers to defend their behaviour on the basis that 'God told me to do it' and all too often the 'message from heaven' is felt to have sufficient authority in itself so that there is no need to check it with the Scriptures. This is no way to grow in holiness. I have known Christians claim divine authority for the most outrageous behaviour. And in over forty years of ministry in the church I have yet to see firm evidence that these extra-biblical 'revelations' have been of lasting benefit to anyone. Not infrequently, they are confused restatements of Scripture and any benefit that accrues could have been obtained by simply reading the word. My personal conviction is that the alarming spread of the cancer of biblical illiteracy – the root cause of our spiritual weakness – is due, at least in some measure, to the current craving. The ignorance gives rise to the craving, and trying to satisfy the craving compounds the ignorance, so that it becomes a vicious circle. The only way to break it is to start taking the Bible seriously. I do not suggest that all who believe in direct revelations are biblically illiterate but even so it is hard to understand why anyone with a thorough working knowledge of the Bible should feel that it is not adequate for the life of faith. What other spiritual resources do we need when the word of God dwells in our hearts? 'I write to you, young men,' says the apostle John, 'because you are strong, and the word of God lives in you' (1 John 2:14).

But although everything we need to know about Christ is contained in the Bible, our relationship is not with the Bible but with the Christ of the Bible. The task of the Holy Spirit is to shed light on the sacred page so that we may apprehend and appreciate the glory of Christ. The spiritual giants of the past, those men and women whose holy lives have made such an impact on our world, understood this. They were all faithful servants of Christ, but the Christ they loved and served was the Christ of the Bible.

To leave this well-trodden highway in the hope of finding something better or something extra, is a sure way of getting hopelessly lost. Let it then be firmly established that understanding God's word is essential if we are to grow in the likeness of Christ. The words of Jesus in his prayer to his Father for his disciples should settle the matter: 'Sanctify them by the truth; your word is truth' (John 17:17).

4. Praying the Word

Praying biblically is a good habit to get into. We may use a single verse as a basis for our prayers. For example, on the basis of Galatians 6:5 mentioned earlier, we could pray: 'Heavenly Father, help me always to remember that I am responsible for my own actions and that one day I shall have to give an account of them before you…' Or we may base our prayers on a longer passage. But we must always take the trouble to make sure we understand the text, because it is so easy to use texts as a peg on which to hang our selfish desires.

The following story will illustrate the ease with which we do this. I was trying to stress the importance of praying biblically to an adult Bible class, using the Lord's Prayer as a model on which to base our petitions and intercessions. I suggested some short prayers and asked the group to tell me which clause, if any, of the Lord's Prayer would sanction them. For example, 'Lord, help me not to try and get my own back…' would be covered by 'as we forgive those who sin against us.' To make the test harder I warned the group that I would throw in some selfish prayers for which no support could be found in the Lord's Prayer, or indeed anywhere else in the Bible. The first one of these was: 'Father, please grant that I may win the lottery…' Without the slightest hesitation, a middle-aged man said: 'Thy will be done'! I felt sorry for the poor man when the rest of the group failed to restrain their amusement.

Obviously, the more we read the word, the better able we shall be to pray in harmony with it, and therefore our prayers will be more and more in line with the will of God. Praying the word will also help us narrow the gap between our creed and conduct.

CHAPTER TEN

Seeing Jesus in Our Suffering

1. Identify the Cause
2. Value the Privilege
3. Maximise the Benefit
4. Avoid False Hopes
5. Avoid Wrong Comparisons
6. Focus on Jesus

'Now if we are children, then we are heirs — heirs of God and co-heirs with Christ, if indeed we share in his sufferings in order that we may also share in his glory'
(Romans 8:17).

1. Identify the Cause

Of all the memories I have of visiting sick and dying people, just a few are more vivid than the rest. One of these goes back to the early years of my ministry, when I was asked to visit a man who was dying from lung cancer. I can still see the tragic scene in his smoke-filled sick-room. The first thing I noticed as I walked in was a large heap of cigarette ends spilling over the sides of an ashtray on the bedside table. The patient, supported by several pillows, was gasping for breath and inhaling the smoke of his cigarette at the same time. After expressing my sympathy for him, I ventured to suggest that it would be a good idea to stop smoking, to which he replied, 'Oh no…it's the only relief I get.' Perhaps the poor man didn't realise when he started smoking what damage it would do, but even so, he could hardly blame anyone but himself. In these circumstances I found it impossible to talk to him about the value of suffering. What sense would it have made?

Looking back over the years, I recall several Christians who were guilty of bringing suffering on themselves. Some were never able to conquer their dreadful addiction to nicotine or alcohol, and their lives were blighted or cut short as a result. Some brought suffering upon themselves (and others) by their bad behaviour; their failure to control the tongue (James 3:5, 6), and even by their sexual immorality. Others endured unnecessary distress by their unwillingness to give up their cherished wilful sins (Psalm 19:13). Suffering caused by the abuse of the human body is common to all, but sin in the believer, when there is no repentance, causes further suffering because God will not permit his redeemed children to be happy in disobedience. The Scriptures provide many examples. When the children of Israel sinned, God sent a plague, or caused them to be defeated in battle (Exodus 32:35; Joshua 7:10-12). When Zechariah, in his old age, doubted God's promise of a son, he was struck dumb for a time (Luke 1:20). And Jonah was thrown overboard in a stormy sea for refusing to obey the Lord's command (Jonah 1:12). No believer refuses to give up cherished sins without suffering the consequences. It is very important then, that we learn not to 'despise the LORD's discipline…because the LORD disciplines those he loves, as a father the son he delights in' (Proverbs 3:11,12).

Ted – not his real name – had to suffer the rude shock of financial loss to make him see that his priorities were all wrong. He was a quiet and friendly family man who worked hard to improve his lot in the world. He professed faith but lacked commitment, and didn't want anything more than a tenuous link with the church. His wife, who was a keen Christian, told me that Ted would work overtime in order to have more money to spend on the latest gadget. One evening he arrived at my door. 'From now on,' he said, 'I want to serve the Lord.' This was music to my ears and I asked Ted what had caused his change of attitude. He replied along these lines: 'I spent a lot of money having the very best stereo equipment fitted into my car, and on Saturday, I left it in one of the city car-parks and took my wife shopping. When I came back an hour or two later, thieves had stripped the lot out.' I asked if he had reported the theft to the police, but wished at once I had not done so, because he was not interested in my question. 'Don't you see,' he said, 'I've been putting material things first for years, and now God has shown me how stupid I've been. I've been saving up for that stereo equipment for a long time, and to see the gaping hole in the dash board was a bitter blow. But it has taught me that it's high time I started getting my priorities right.' 'What does Vera, your wife, think about it? I asked. 'Oh' said Ted, 'she's still thanking the Lord the stuff was pinched.'

It is not always easy of course, to ascertain the cause of our suffering and we must not jump to conclusions. But if the affliction raises a question mark over something in our own lives that we have an uneasy conscience about, the only sensible thing to do is to repent of it and forsake it. If we find this hard to do, we must pray for a still deeper repentance. We must never give in to it.

2. Value the Privilege

Melting gold in order to refine it is a very ancient craft. It was well-known in ancient Israel; the vessels of the tabernacle and the temple being made of pure gold. The unrefined metal was placed in a furnace until it melted. In this state it was easy to remove the impurities. The use of the process as an illustration of God's purpose in putting his people through fiery trials in order to remove the dross in their character, is also very ancient. We have an example of it in the words of Job to his would-be comforters: 'But he knows the way that I take; when he has tested me, I shall come forth as gold' (Job 23:10). Two further examples are to be found in the Book of Proverbs: 'The crucible for silver and the furnace for gold, but the LORD tests the heart' (Proverbs 17:3). 'The crucible for silver and the furnace for gold, but man is tested by the praise he receives' (Proverbs 27:21).

This is as true today as it ever was. God still sends suffering to his people for the purpose of refining their character and strengthening their faith. Referring to the trials believers are called upon to endure, the apostle Peter says: 'These have come so that your faith

– of greater worth than gold, which perishes even though refined by fire – may be proved genuine and may result in praise, glory and honour when Jesus Christ is revealed' (1 Peter 1:7). Taking careful notice of what Peter is saying here will not only set us free from a plaintive spirit, but will also help us to understand what privileged people we are. God does not send trials to knock us down, but to build us up. As Derek Kidner puts it, in his commentary on the Book of Proverbs: God's 'trials are...not for finding a person out but for sorting him out' (Tyndale New Testament Commentaries, page 123). We cannot be sure whether Peter is thinking of the 'praise and honour' the Lord will give to those whose faith is proved genuine, or whether it is we who will give praise and honour to Christ by proving that he is worthy of our trust. Either way, it is the Lord who is glorified. What better outcome can there be?

All our sufferings then must be seen as the Lord's discipline, remembering always that he is weaning us from an inordinate love of the world by making us realise its vanity and its transitory nature, and training us for the glory to come. It must therefore also be seen as a privilege to be greatly valued. Every child of God should take to heart the words of the writer to the Hebrews: 'My son, do not make light of the Lord's discipline, and do not lose heart when he rebukes you, because the Lord disciplines those whom he loves, and he punishes everyone he accepts as a son.' The writer goes on to remind us that 'no discipline seems pleasant at the time, but painful. Later on, however, it produces a harvest of righteousness and peace for those who have been trained by it' (Hebrews 12:5, 6, 11). The last few words are important. The harvest of righteousness is reaped by those who learn to use their afflictions to promote holiness. Those who see no purpose in them, gain no benefit from them.

How easily we become too attached to this age! But how much more easily we would do so, if our sense of physical or financial well-being were never disturbed! That would be a tragedy of the worst kind, because the love of this world is a hindrance to our progress in faith. Loving the world and trying to grow in the likeness of Christ at the same time is like trying to drive a car without releasing the hand-brake. The engine always stalls! 'Do not love the world' says John, 'or anything in the world. If anyone loves the world, the love of the Father is not in him' (1 John 2:15). 'If heaven is our country, what can the earth be but a place of exile?' (Calvin, *Institutes*, Book 3, chapter 9, paragraph 4).

So when we are called to endure hardship, let us see it as the gracious chastisement of a loving Father. 'We have all had human fathers who disciplined us and we respected them for it. How much more should we submit to the Father of our spirits and live! Our fathers disciplined us for a little while as they thought best; but God disciplines us for our good, that we may share in his holiness' (Hebrews 12:9-10). What a privilege!

In the light of this, it is sheer folly for believers to refuse to accept the inevitability of suffering as some are inclined to do. Apart from the fact that this attitude wilfully ignores the stark reality that everyone born into this world endures suffering, it also fails to take Scripture seriously. We know that God created everything good (Genesis 1:31) and that suffering is an intrusion caused by the entrance of sin into the world. We also know that pain and death are the result of the curse under which the whole creation languishes (Genesis 3:15-19). In the new Jerusalem we shall be free from the curse (Revelation 21:4) but in the meantime we must suffer like the rest. Believers who entertain the hope that they may be exempt will not avoid disillusionment, and will deprive themselves of rich blessings. In addition to the suffering we have to endure that is common to humanity, Christians will also suffer persecution – suffering that cannot be avoided except by being unfaithful and hiding our lamp under a bowl (Matthew 5:15).

To avoid this error, Scripture must shape our thinking. From its teaching we learn that, as believers, we are called to suffer with Christ. If we shrink in horror from the idea, it proves that we have not yet understood what Christian discipleship is all about. The words of the apostle Peter will act as a corrective: 'But if you suffer for doing good and you endure it, this is commendable before God. To this you were called, because Christ suffered for you, leaving you an example that you should follow in his steps' (1 Peter 2:20b-21). Some may want to argue that since Peter was addressing slaves, this does not apply to all believers. But the calling to which the apostle refers is the calling into the Christian family that we all receive, and he is making the point that suffering will be our lot whatever our circumstances. Christian slaves, just like the rest of God's people, should see their suffering as part of their calling. Paul too will set us right: 'I want to know Christ and the power of his resurrection, and the fellowship of his sufferings, becoming like him in his death…' (Philippians 3:10). Here the apostle is saying that he actually longs to enter more fully into the afflictions of Christ. He sees the experience as vital to his own spiritual development, which he defines as 'becoming like Jesus in his death.' What he means is this: just as Jesus died to sin (in the sense that by his death he is now free from the burden of our sin), Paul wanted to die to sin (his own). We too should long to be like Jesus in his death. For if we are not willing for our sins to be crucified (the sins for which he was crucified), how can we claim to be his followers? If we are unwilling to suffer with Christ, how can we claim to have an interest in being like him?

Paul's conviction that the Lord allowed him to suffer so that the glory of Jesus might be revealed through him is quite moving: 'We always carry around in our body the death of Jesus,' he says, 'so that the life of Jesus may also be revealed in our body' (2 Corinthians 4:10). The apostle knew many believers, both Jews and Gentiles, and he was keenly aware of the fact that they all suffered for the sake of Christ. And he, always conscious of his weakness, was persecuted and in constant danger. And yet his only concern was to glorify Jesus. Although the lesson is so obvious, it seems to have been largely overlooked.

In Romans chapter six, Paul shows that the source and guarantee of true holiness is our oneness with the Lord Jesus Christ. 'If we have been united with him in his death, we will certainly also be united with him in his resurrection' (Romans 6:5). Just as Christ's death was followed by the certainty of his resurrection, so those who belong to him will just as surely die to sin and rise to a new life of holiness. The implications are obvious. Our death to sin and our growth in his likeness cannot be achieved without pain. Because of our union with Christ, his sufferings 'flow over into our lives' (2 Corinthians 1:5). How misguided then are those who think they can be joined to Christ and escape suffering! We are 'co-heirs with Christ, if indeed we share in his sufferings in order that we may also share in his glory' (Romans 8:17).

Jesus was referring to this aspect of suffering when he told his disciples: 'You will drink the cup I drink and be baptised with the baptism I am baptised with...' (Mark 10:39). And again, when he said: 'If anyone would come after me, he must deny himself and take up his cross and follow me' (Mark 8:34). Since Christ was without sin, his sufferings were entirely undeserved, and being one with him, we too will suffer unjustly. Since this is the way the Master went; must not the servant tread it still? Those who are committed to the cause of the gospel will know what it means to suffer for doing good. 'In fact, everyone who wants to live a godly life in Christ Jesus will be persecuted' (2 Timothy 3:12).

In one church of which I was minister, a goodly number of long-standing members resented the message I preached, and were clearly irritated by the presence of new converts in the church. My insistence on the new birth was seen as 'new-fangled teaching.' Consequently, as soon as people turned to Christ and became committed to the church, they were immediately persecuted. Anonymous and threatening letters were sent by people who claimed to be faithful members of the church (which, contrary to my fears, had the effect of strengthening the young believers.) One letter I remember consigned me to the fires of hell! Over the telephone I was told, by persons whose voices I recognised, what an unfit person I was to be a minister, but they would not repeat their criticisms in public. This kind of hostile opposition lasted for some time, and since rumours were circulating that I was immoral, and I had evidence that attempts to frame me might be made, I could no longer make myself available for interviews at the church when no one else was present, as had been my custom. Interviews with members of the opposite sex whom I did not know or could not trust were conducted with my study door open and my wife not far away. Compared with the persecution suffered by believers in other lands, this is nothing, but it demonstrates the antagonism to the gospel wherever it is proclaimed, and to those who proclaim it. It also shows that the enemies of the gospel are all too often in the religious establishment – just as they were in Jesus' day.

Far from regarding suffering then as evil, the Bible sees it as a precious gift that God uses for our good. 'Blessed is the man who perseveres under trial,' says James, 'because when he has stood the test, he will receive the crown of life that God has promised to those who love him' (James 1:12). 'For it has been granted to you on behalf of Christ not only to believe on him, but also to suffer for him' (Philippians 1:29). Once we understand this, suffering in all its forms takes on a totally new meaning.

A few years ago I had the unpleasant experience of meeting a couple who believed Christians should never suffer. They saw disease in any form, not as a test of faith, but as evidence of the lack of it. My wife and I were staying in what was advertised as a Christian guest house and the lady of the house discovered that I was suffering from the after-effects of a heart-attack. Without making any enquiry about my medical or spiritual history, she lectured me about the need for faith and put me under pressure to allow her to lay hands on me. When I politely declined she evidently did not like it, and a few days later when we were leaving, she informed my wife that I was under the devil's curse! If only the lady had known how many times over the years I have had to minister to Christians whose distress had been aggravated by such people. My wife, knowing I would be angry, did not pass the information on to me until we had left the house. So I wrote to the lady explaining why it is not possible for believers to fall under the curse of the devil, but she did not take the trouble to reply.

'Ah but', someone will say, 'did Jesus not say that everything is possible for him who believes' (Mark 9:23)? Indeed, he did, and it is a gospel principle without which the Christian faith would not make sense. But we must understand that by using the word 'everything' Jesus certainly did not mean things that are outside the will of God. Again, some will object that this is a devious attempt to evade the problem, but if so, why did God refuse Paul's request to remove the 'thorn in the flesh' (2 Corinthians 12:7-10)? Was he lacking in faith, or was there some other reason? The record clearly shows that there was indeed another reason, and as a direct result the apostle was greatly blessed. It is a serious mistake to think God's gift of faith may be used to alter his will.

A wrong attitude to Christian suffering however is not just the fault of a few zealots. One could be forgiven for thinking that most gospel preachers these days have taken a vow to keep silent on the subject. It seems potential converts must be kept ignorant of it at all costs; otherwise they might change their minds about following Jesus. Popular courses on Christian discipleship remain silent about it as well, and for the same reason. In stark contrast, we read that Paul and Barnabas made a special point of it. They 'returned to Lystra, Iconium and Antioch, strengthening the disciples and encouraging them to remain true to the faith. "We must go through many hardships to enter the kingdom of God," they said' (Acts 14:21-22. See also Acts 9:16).

We do believe that God will heal our physical diseases and deliver us from severe trials if he so chooses, as many of us can testify. And we would be very ungrateful not to thank him for it. By so doing, we are acknowledging that it is God's work, no matter what means were used. Not many of us need to be convinced of his ability to do this, but we need to balance this belief with a firm conviction of the privilege and value of suffering. Let us ask the Lord for grace to learn this lesson.

'How powerfully', says Calvin, 'should it soften the bitterness of the cross, to think that the more we are afflicted with adversity, the surer we are made of our fellowship with God; by communion with whom our sufferings are not only blessed to us, but tend greatly to the furtherance of our salvation' (Calvin, Institutes, Book 3, chapter 8).

3. Maximise the Benefit

The spiritual benefits of physical suffering are not always immediate. Sometimes, during severe trials and in spite of our efforts to read and pray, God seems remote, the heavens seem like brass, and we feel deserted. It is only as we recover, that the precious lessons begin to dawn on us. Only a matter of months ago, I suffered what was, without doubt, the strangest illness of my life. It started with a severe pain in the abdomen which soon began to ease with medication, only to be replaced by acute insomnia and frequent panic attacks. The longer it went on, the less I was able to cope, until I reached the point where feelings of despair were beginning to creep in. It was extremely difficult to turn my mind to anything for more than a few minutes at a time. The words of Psalm 73 come near to describing my experience: 'But as for me, my feet had almost slipped; I had nearly lost my foothold... all day long I have been plagued; I have been punished every morning... When my heart was grieved and my spirit embittered, I was senseless and ignorant; I was a brute beast before you. Yet I am always with you; you hold me by my right hand. You guide me with your counsel; and afterward you will take me into glory' (verses 2, 14, 21-24). With gratitude to God and in humility, I think I can say that since I recovered, the privilege of being a child of God has thrilled my soul as never before. And this is by no means the first time this has happened. Therefore I cannot assume that my faith cannot be strengthened even further by such experiences, even though I do not relish the thought of it.

If I may add another confession, it is because of my inability to rejoice in the Lord more during trials that I always feel a little uncomfortable with Philippians 4:4-7. 'Rejoice in the Lord always. I will say it again: Rejoice!... Do not be anxious about anything; but in everything, by prayer and petition, with thanksgiving, present your requests to God. And the peace of God, which transcends all understanding, will guard your hearts and your minds in Christ Jesus.' It is probably because the command to rejoice always seems so unreasonable that Paul repeats it. But how can we possibly rejoice when we are in pain, or distress? After all, the writer to the Hebrews acknowledges that discipline is unpleasant. But the fact that the apostle commands us to rejoice at all times proves that it is not impossible. The rejoicing does not of course suddenly replace the suffering, but co-exists with it and afterwards is enhanced by it.

We need also to remember, as we saw in chapter seven, that we do not rejoice because of our sufferings. This mistaken idea became popular some years ago, and several Christians in the church where I was serving adopted it. To make statements like 'Praise the Lord, my wife has left me' or 'I'm rejoicing because I've got cancer' is too ridiculous for words. We rejoice in the Lord because by his grace we shall soon enjoy that new order in which there will be 'no more death or mourning or crying or pain' (Revelation 21:4), and not because we are suffering. Indeed, a strong assurance of future glory is vital if we are to improve our ability to rejoice always. Paul preserves this connection in Romans 5:2, 3: 'And we rejoice in the hope of the glory of God. Not only so, but we also rejoice in our sufferings, because we know that suffering produces perseverance; perseverance, character; and character, hope.' The stronger our hope in heaven, the healthier our attitude to suffering will be.

4. Avoid False Hopes

The following true stories illustrate the folly of thinking that faith should always be the means of deliverance from suffering and that sooner or later, if we persist in it, the idea will lead to self-deception. I once preached a sermon during the course of which I made it clear that as far as believers are concerned, God both sends and uses suffering to accomplish his will in us. I cited the case of Paul's 'thorn in the flesh' (2 Corinthians 12:7-10), and the Lord's words to Saul of Tarsus via Ananias: 'I will show him how much he must suffer for my name' (Acts 9:16). A member of my congregation had been taught by another minister that it is never God's will for Christians to suffer, and she could not understand how 'two men of God could disagree on such an important subject' (her words to me at a later stage). Unknown to me, she wrote to the minister in question with details of my sermon. Imagine my surprise when, a few days later, I received a lengthy letter from him pointing out my error! Some leaflets were enclosed which had been written by my correspondent. Among the first words that caught my eye were these: 'Let's get this straight from the very beginning – it is never God's will for Christians to suffer.' Many years later I was on holiday with my wife and we went to worship at the local church, and the same minister was the guest preacher. Imagine our astonishment when we discovered that he was still proclaiming the same message even though he had to sit down to preach. There was something wrong with his back and he was evidently in pain!

A young woman, who believed that suffering in believers was always due to a lack of faith, fell sick. She looked pale and had a hacking cough. I began to express my regret, but before I could get the words out she sharply rebuked me. Clearly angered by my suggestion that she was ill, she said: 'The Lord has healed me. It's just that he hasn't yet taken away the symptoms.' If such self-deception were not so serious it would be laughable. I could say no more, but privately I was aghast that anyone could be so naive. I guess the lady was basing her confidence on the Lord's words in Mark 11:23: 'I tell you the truth, if anyone says to this mountain, 'Go throw yourself into the sea,' and does not doubt in his heart but believes that what he says will happen, it will be done for him. Therefore I tell you, whatever you ask in prayer, believe that you have received it, and it will be yours.' It will be seen at once that Jesus did not expect us to take the 'mountain' literally. Mountains are symbols for apparently insurmountable difficulties (See Zechariah 4:7) which God can remove in response to faith. It will also be obvious that the words 'believe that you have received it' do not give us the right to demand whatever we want, when we want it. In any case, it is only when we ask for things that are in accordance with the perfect will of God for us, that we may be sure of an affirmative answer (1 John 5:14) and even then we may have to wait for it. By faith we believe we have already been given an inheritance in heaven, but we are still here!

By contrast, I was talking to a Christian lady who has been suffering from Spondylosis for years. I was expressing my sympathy for her but before I could finish, she too interrupted. With a beaming smile and evidently with great feeling, she said, 'Oh, but I am looking forward to my new resurrection body.' What a difference! She evidently believed she had already received a title to the glory to come, but she also knew the difference between what has been called the 'now' and the 'not yet.' I think we would all have to admit that such patient confidence is rare today.

The trumpeted claims of those who believe in continuous perfect health in response to faith begin to sound very hollow when they have to face the fact of death. The last enemy, not to be abolished until Christ returns (1 Corinthians 15:26), will come to us all if the Lord tarries. Sad to say however, even when death strikes some still refuse to face facts. Instead of being honest and admitting their mistake, they stand logic on its head by insisting that death is the perfect healing they have been talking about and therefore their claims are proven! Asked why people die if there is nothing wrong with them, they insist that they just die. Presumably, in this case, the doctor would have to invent the cause of death, or leave the death certificate blank. May the Lord deliver us from such lamentable self-deception!

5. Avoid Wrong Comparisons

Picture an old pair of scales, like the ones Grandma used to use. What would happen if we put a feather on one side and a heavy weight on the other? The heavy side would go down with a bump. Now, think of the feather as representing our present sufferings and the heavy weight as a symbol of the glory to come. Paul may have had a similar picture in mind when he said: 'For our light and momentary troubles are achieving for us an eternal weight of glory that far outweighs them all' (2 Corinthians 4:17). Again in Romans 8:18, he says: 'I consider that our present sufferings are not worth comparing with the glory that will be revealed in us.' If these words had come from the pen of someone with little experience of suffering, we might have been tempted to say he didn't know what he was talking about. But Paul knew more about suffering than most of us. He was stoned, beaten, whipped, robbed, and shipwrecked. He was poor and homeless and in almost constant danger (2 Corinthians 11:24-29), and it seems he did not enjoy good health either. On one occasion he tells us that the pressure he was under was far beyond his ability to bear it. So much so that he despaired even of life (2 Corinthians 1:8). In comparison with the experience of most people, the apostle's sufferings were anything but light. But Paul was not in the habit of comparing his afflictions with those of the people around him, as we do so often. ('You can always find others worse than yourself' is a common observation.) His heart was set on the things above where Christ is seated at the right hand of God, and so much so that in comparison with them, he could not help but see his current afflictions as light. He did not lose heart, because his eyes were fixed, 'not on what is seen, but on what is unseen' (2 Corinthians 4:18). He knew that 'though outwardly we are wasting away, yet inwardly we are being renewed day by day' (2 Corinthians 4:16).

6. Focus on Jesus

Knowing he was about to face death on a trumped up charge, Stephen, 'full of the Holy Spirit, looked up to heaven and saw the glory of God, and Jesus standing at the right hand of God. "Look," he said, "I see heaven open and the Son of Man standing at the right hand of God"' (Acts 7:55, 56). God was very gracious to his suffering servant to grant him this glimpse of glory, and we must see this as an exceptional case. But we should understand that this heavenly-minded man was well instructed in the Old Testament Scriptures, and had made a habit of fixing his eyes on Jesus. The glory he saw with his own eyes that day, he had been accustomed to seeing with the eye of faith every day. His likeness to his Lord, seen so clearly in his defence, and in his prayer for his persecutors, could not have been achieved otherwise (Acts 7). Like Stephen, many believers have proved at the end of their lives on this earth (even though they did not see visions), that there is a strong link between a faithful life and a triumphant death. None of us can be sure just how we shall die, but there is plenty of evidence to prove that those who face death with confidence have been in the habit of focusing on Jesus during their sufferings. If we do not cultivate that habit, we must not expect to develop it suddenly in the hour of death.

Here then is the secret of rejoicing in our suffering. We develop the habit of meditating daily on the glory of Jesus – glory that we shall soon share, when all suffering will be a thing of the past. Peter's encouraging words are as relevant now as the day they were written: 'Dear friends, do not be surprised at the painful trial you are suffering, as though something strange were happening to you.

But rejoice that you participate in the sufferings of Christ, so that you may be overjoyed when his glory is revealed' (1 Peter 4:12, 13). 'Consider him who endured such opposition from sinful men, so that you will not grow weary and lose heart' (Hebrews 12:3). It is for lack of this regular consideration that many believers are soon discouraged, and have no confidence in the face of death.

THE GLORY TO COME

CHAPTER ELEVEN

The Glory of His Return

1. He is coming in Person
2. He is coming in Public
3. He is coming in Glory
4. He is coming for His Own

'At that time the sign of the Son of Man will appear in the sky, and all the nations of the earth will mourn. They will see the Son of Man coming on the clouds of the sky, with power and great glory'
Matthew 24:30.

The day of the Lord's return is the day of final judgment when the dead will be raised and the wicked separated from the righteous (Matthew 13:49, 50). It is the day when all the powers that oppose God's redemptive purposes will be destroyed (2 Thessalonians 2:8). It is the day on which the lowly bodies of all who belong to Christ will be transformed 'so that they will be like his glorious body' (Philippians 3:21). It is the day when every tear will be wiped away because the causes of weeping will be abolished forever (Revelation 21:1-4). It is the day of our full redemption, when the glory of Christ we now see but dimly, will be fully revealed, and our joy, now marred by sorrow and sin, will be complete. It is the day when Jesus will come 'to be glorified in his holy people and to be marvelled at among all those who have believed' (2 Thessalonians 1:10).

1. He is coming in Person

In May 1944 I was 'on parade' with thousands of soldiers of the 79th Armoured Division, in a huge field somewhere in the county of Suffolk, England. We were standing in ranks round the four sides of the field, waiting for the arrival of Field Marshal Montgomery. After what seemed like an age, he arrived in a jeep and directed his driver to stop in the centre of the field. Dispensing with military formalities, he climbed onto the bonnet of the jeep and signalled to the troops to gather round the vehicle. We listened as he, in his flamboyant manner, talked about the forthcoming invasion of Europe.

As we waited in that field, everyone expected 'Monty' (as he was known) to arrive soon and in person. That is exactly what we had been told by our senior officers, and we had no reason whatever to doubt it. They were reliable men, and even though we waited much longer than expected, we did not begin to think that perhaps we had been deceived and that the Field Marshal was not really coming in person after all. Nor did we begin to feel that the order to assemble to meet him had some figurative or hidden meaning. It would be rather difficult, to say the least, to maintain a disciplined army if its soldiers started to interpret orders in this way.

What then, are we to think of Christians, or people who say they are Christians, who do not believe the plain statements of Scripture that Jesus is coming again in person, even though they were written by honest and trustworthy men who 'spoke from God' (2 Peter 1:21)? If the New Testament contained no more than just one or two ambiguous references to the personal return of Christ, the doubters may have some excuse, but there are over three hundred of them, and only a very few could be called ambiguous. Yet we are told that all these texts are merely figurative, or even that the writers were mistaken! Perhaps the most popular suggestion is that they all speak of Christ coming again at death. But this is to accuse the writers of deceit. How is it possible, for example, to interpret what Luke tells us in Acts 1:11 in this way? After describing the bodily ascension of Jesus which took place before the 'very eyes' of the apostles, '...two men dressed in white stood beside them. "Men of Galilee," they said, "why do you stand here looking into the sky? This same Jesus, who has been taken from you into heaven, will come back in the same way you have seen him go into heaven."' Where is the evidence that Luke was speaking figuratively, or that he was mistaken? All the evidence shows that he was a first class historian. In the prologue to his Gospel he says: 'Many have undertaken to draw up an account of the things that have been fulfilled among us, just as they were handed down to us by those who from the first were eye-witnesses and servants of the word. Therefore, since I myself have carefully investigated everything from the beginning, it seemed good also to me to write an orderly account for you, most excellent Theophilus, so that you may know the certainty of the things you have been taught' (Luke 1:1-4). Does this sound like a man who was mistaken or who would conceal a hidden meaning behind what purports to be a historical account? How then can intelligent and well-educated people say the Scriptures do not speak of a personal return of the Lord Jesus Christ? The two men in white who appeared to the apostles seemed to go out of their way to prevent such an interpretation. They announced that the same Jesus will come back in the same way.

As we have seen, the Bible writers did not intend us to take everything they wrote literally, but with few exceptions, it is obvious which passages are literal and which are not. There is not the slightest hint anywhere in Scripture that the promises of the Lord's personal return are anything other than literal and it is an insult to the intelligence to suggest otherwise. Would it not be more honourable for these manipulators to admit they just do not believe it?

Space will not permit us to refer to more than a few of the many verses. Take first the words of Jesus himself: 'At that time the sign of the Son of Man will appear in the sky, and all the nations of the earth will mourn. They will see the Son of Man coming on the clouds of the sky...' (Matthew 24:30). Some scholars have argued that even these words are symbolic and cannot refer to the second coming because the prophecy on which they are based (Daniel 7:13) speaks of 'one like a son of man, coming with the clouds of heaven' but does not say that he comes to earth. But we have already seen that this is how the 'two men dressed in white' spoke of his coming (Acts

2:11). It is also the way the apostle John speaks of it: 'Look, he is coming with the clouds, and every eye will see him, even those who pierced him; and all the peoples of the earth will mourn because of him. So shall it be! Amen' (Revelation 1:7).

Paul too speaks of his coming in person. 'But our citizenship is in heaven' he says, 'And we eagerly await a Saviour from there, the Lord Jesus Christ' (Philippians 3:20) Writing to the Christians in Thessalonica, the apostle looks forward to the day when he will rejoice with them in the presence of the Lord Jesus: 'For what is our hope, our joy, or the crown in which we will glory in the presence of our Lord Jesus Christ when he comes?' He also looks forward to receiving his reward when Jesus appears in person. 'Now there is in store for me the crown of righteousness, which the Lord, the righteous Judge, will award to me on that day – and not only to me, but also to all who have longed for his appearing' (2 Timothy 4:8).

2. He is coming in Public

The religious sect known as 'Jehovah's Witnesses' teach that Jesus came secretly in 1874 and in power in 1914. At least, that was his intention, but when he arrived the people did not repent as they should have done, so he went into hiding, waiting for a more favourable time! Their position cannot be maintained, not least because God does not make blunders, nor is he taken by surprise by the reaction of people. In any case, the Bible is explicit that Jesus is coming back in public. There is no evidence whatever to suggest that Jesus has already come, nor does the Bible have anything to say about a secret coming.

But do not many Christians believe in a secret coming? Indeed they do. The 'secret rapture' as it is called, used to be a very popular idea. The idea is that there are two comings (some think more) – Jesus 'coming for his saints' as distinct from his later 'coming with his saints.' He does not actually come to this earth the first time, but believers, living or dead, their bodies now made glorious and imperishable, are taken up to meet the Lord in the air. The teaching is mistakenly based on texts like Revelation 20:4, 5: 'They came to life and reigned with Christ a thousand years. (The rest of the dead did not come to life until the thousand years were ended.) This is the first resurrection.' But surely John is talking here about those who are now living and reigning with Christ in heaven, the thousand years being symbolic of the present period of Christ's reign. Unlike the historical narratives of the Gospels and the Acts of the Apostles, the Book of Revelation is highly symbolic. 'The rest of the dead' – those who did not believe – will not be raised until the end of this age when Christ returns, and then only for judgment.

Further support is claimed for the idea of a secret coming in 1 Thessalonians 4:13-18, which tells us that 'the dead in Christ will rise first. After that, we who are still alive and are left will be caught up with them in the clouds to meet the Lord in the air.' This is supposed to mean that when believers, both dead and living, are 'caught up,' they will simply disappear from the face of the earth.

The idea has been depicted by an artist, whose picture was popular fifty or sixty years ago. I remember seeing it hanging in the home of some Christian friends. It portrayed the Lord in the sky and believers robed in white ascending from fields, from buildings, from trains and so forth. Whenever I saw the picture I was left wondering what the people who were left would think about the sudden disappearance of so many people, and how they would cope with the crisis that would inevitably follow. Presumably, if both the pilot and co-pilot of a jumbo jet flying at thirty thousand feet were believers, the aircraft would crash, killing all the rest of the people on board!

Some point to Matthew 24:40, 41, in support of this interpretation. Jesus said: 'Two men will be in the field; one will be taken and the other left. Two women will be grinding with a handmill; one will be taken and the other left.' But surely the point Jesus is making is that when he returns a permanent separation will take place between believers and unbelievers, even though they may have been in a close relationship in this life. As Bishop Ryle puts it: 'Wives shall be separated from husbands, parents from children, brothers from sisters, masters from servants, preachers from hearers. There shall be no time for repentance, or a change of mind, when the Lord appears: all shall be taken as they are, and reap according as they have sown' (Expository Thoughts on the Gospels).

It is true that at the Lord's return the Christian 'dead will be raised imperishable, and that those who are alive when the Lord returns will be changed 'in a flash' (1 Corinthians 15:52). It is also true that we shall all be 'caught up' together to meet the Lord in the clouds (1 Thessalonians 4:17). But none of this will take place in secret. Paul shows that on the very same day that the Lord is 'revealed from heaven in blazing fire with his powerful angels,' he will put an end to the persecution of his people (2 Thessalonians 1:6, 7). And on the same day, he will banish from his presence all who 'do not obey the gospel' (2 Thessalonians 1:8).

The same day is still in mind when the apostle warns his readers 'not to become easily unsettled or alarmed by some prophecy, report or letter supposed to have come from us, saying that the day of the Lord has already come. Don't let anyone deceive you in any way for that day will not come until the rebellion occurs and the man of lawlessness is revealed, the man doomed to destruction' (2 Thessalonians 2:2-3). Now why would Paul warn them about these very public signs if the Lord's coming is to be in secret? Why would he talk about the rebellion and destruction of the man of lawlessness, if he believed in a secret coming? And even if he did believe it, would he not have pointed to the fact that none of the Thessalonian believers had disappeared as evidence for the falsehood of the reports? If they had been true, there would have been no believers to write letters to, and no apostle to write them! The idea of a secret coming simply does not fit.

The apostle Peter agrees. The Lord is patient with his own, says Peter, not wanting any to perish, and in the next breath he says, 'But the day of the Lord will come like a thief. The heavens will disappear with a roar, the elements will be destroyed by fire, and the earth and everything in it will be laid bare' (2 Peter 3:10). No mention of any secret coming here. Some have suggested that the words 'like a thief' indicate a secret coming, but this is absurd. The words simply mean 'without warning.' Thieves don't send e-mails to say when they are calling. We affirm then, that the Lord Jesus is coming in person and in public on a day known only to God himself.

3. He is coming in Glory

From the verses of Scripture already quoted we cannot fail to see that Jesus is not only coming in person and in public; he is also coming in power and great glory. He is not coming as a servant to suffer, but as a King to reign. He is not coming to take a body that is mortal, but in his glorious and incorruptible body. He is not coming to be laid in a manger in the care of Mary and Joseph, but on the clouds of heaven with powerful angels in his train (2 Thessalonians 1:7). He is not coming to die, but to destroy death (1 Corinthians 15:26). 'I saw heaven standing open' says John, 'and there before me was a white horse, whose rider is called Faithful and True. With justice he judges and makes war. His eyes are like blazing fire, and on his head are many crowns. He has a name written on him that no one but he himself knows. He is dressed in a robe dipped in blood, and his name is the Word of God. The armies of heaven were following him, riding on white horses and dressed in fine linen, white and clean. Out of his mouth comes a sharp sword with which to strike down the nations. "He will rule them with an iron sceptre." He treads the winepress of the fury of the wrath of God Almighty. On his robe and on his thigh he has this name written: KING OF KINGS AND LORD OF LORDS' (Revelation 19:11-16). For all the vivid imagery, it cannot be disputed that here is a vision of Christ. The names 'Faithful and True,' the 'Word of God' (John 1:1), and the 'KING OF KINGS,' cannot apply to anyone else. We see him coming with the angels in irresistible power to destroy his enemies and to set up his eternal kingdom on earth, over which he will reign supreme. No anti-Christian power will withstand the fury of his wrath (Revelation 16:19).

Paul corroborates this. Speaking of the coming judgment of God on those who persecute his children the apostle says: 'This will happen when the Lord Jesus is revealed from heaven in blazing fire with his powerful angels. He will punish those who do not know God and do not obey the gospel of our Lord Jesus. They will be punished with everlasting destruction and shut out from the presence of the Lord and from the majesty of his power on the day he comes to be glorified in his holy people and to be marvelled at among all those who have believed' (2 Thessalonians 1:7-10). If you are like me, these words will fill you with fear and joy at the same time; fear for those who refuse to repent and believe; fear for those we love who are still holding out against Christ; and joy because the day is coming when we shall see Jesus. On that day, as the hymnwriter puts it, we shall be 'lost in wonder, love and praise,' and the perfect glory of our beloved Lord will be seen in us.

4. He is coming for His Own

The Scriptures compare the Second Advent to a wedding. To understand the passages where this occurs we need to understand the marriage customs of the Jews in New Testament times. In the west (although there may sometimes be exceptions) it is usual for the man to propose to the woman, and if she says 'yes', the engagement follows. This may last for weeks, months, or even years. A broken engagement may cause heartbreak but it does not usually lead to legal action for breach of promise. If all goes well, the marriage ceremony, which is legally binding, takes place, followed by the reception and the honeymoon. The marriage customs of the Jews were different. The 'engagement' was a formal arrangement between the father of the bride and the father of the bridegroom. This was followed immediately by the 'betrothal, during which promises were made in the presence of witnesses. Like our marriage service, this ceremony was legally binding and any cancellation of the agreement was seen as divorce. A year elapsed before the actual marriage. The marriage celebrations took place at the bridegroom's home after he and his friends had gone in procession to fetch his wife from her parents' house. The celebrations could go on for several days.

Jesus the Lamb of God is the 'Bridegroom' and the true church his 'bride'. 'Then I heard what sounded like a great multitude,' says John, 'like the roar of rushing waters and like loud peals of thunder, shouting: "Hallelujah! For our Lord God Almighty reigns. Let us rejoice and be glad and give him the glory! For the wedding of the lamb has come, and his bride has made herself ready. Fine linen, bright and clean was given her to wear." (Fine linen stands for the righteous acts of the saints)' (Revelation 19:6-8). Since we are already 'betrothed' to Christ – in a covenant that cannot be broken – and since his second advent is seen as the marriage (followed by a never-ending celebration!), we must see the period in which we now live as the time when his bride, the church, is making herself ready for the glory to come. It is not difficult to imagine how the bride felt as she looked forward to the coming of the one she loved, and what care she would take to be looking her best. After all, this was the fulfilment of her hope and desire.

And shall not we, who look forward to the coming of the one we love, regard our lives here and now as a preparation for his appearance? After all, this is one of the main reasons why these wonderful future events are revealed to us. And if we really love him, shall we not long for his appearing (2 Timothy 4:8)? The fact is, however that many of us are so caught up with treasure on earth and the affairs of this life, that we know little or nothing of that longing.

When I was quite young in the faith, this sad situation troubled me so much, for I was drawn to the teaching that when the Lord returns the church would be split in two – those who are looking for him and those who are not. Those who are looking for him would be caught up with him, but those who are not would be left behind. I was influenced by a Bible writer, well-known at the time, who taught that this was the meaning of the parable of the ten virgins. The ten girls went out to meet the bridegroom coming for his bride, but five were wise and five were foolish. The foolish bridesmaids did not take any oil in their lamps. The bridegroom was a long time coming and all ten fell asleep. At midnight the cry rang out: 'Here's the bridegroom! Come out to meet him.' The lamps of the foolish five were going out, and they begged the wise ones to give them some of their oil, but were refused. While they were on their way to buy some oil, the bridegroom arrived and the five wise girls went into the wedding banquet. Later on, the foolish ones asked to be allowed in but the door was shut and they were refused entry. 'I tell you the truth' said the bridegroom, 'I don't know you' (Matthew 25:1-13). My understanding of the parable seemed to me to be backed up by Hebrews 9:28: '…so Christ was sacrificed once to take way the sins of many people, and he will appear a second time, not to bear sin, but to bring salvation to those who are waiting for him.' Are there not many believers I asked myself, who, like the five foolish virgins, are not waiting for him?

At the time, it all seemed so convincing, but it will not stand up to scrutiny. The parable of the ten virgins simply makes the point that true believers are wise and will be ready for the Lord's return. Not one of his own people will be left outside the door. The foolish virgins must therefore be seen as people for whom Jesus did not 'bring salvation'; who discover when it is too late that they are not ready, people who may profess to belong to Christ, but are not truly born of the Spirit and have no place at the marriage feast. In other words, the distinguishing feature of those to whom Christ brings salvation is that they are 'waiting for him'. The parable does not focus on the fate of those who were not ready. It simply makes the point that those who belong to him are expecting and preparing for his coming.

We can therefore rejoice in the fact that many true believers, who are slack in this matter, will be safe when Jesus comes again. But we cannot rejoice in the fact that in the meantime they will be deprived of many blessings. Their incentive to grow in holiness will be weak, and they will know little or nothing about the assurance of salvation. How much wiser are they who fix their eyes on the coming Lord, and are preparing to meet him! Those who do so will be always growing in confidence. Those who don't will be ashamed at his coming. The possibility of believers being ashamed is hinted at by John the apostle: 'And now dear children, continue in him, so that when he appears we may be confident and unashamed before him at his coming' (1 John 2:28). The power to 'continue in him' is, of course, given by God alone, but the apostle's words make it clear that this does not relieve us of the responsibility to work at it. Our aim is to be 'blameless and holy in the presence of our God and Father when our Lord Jesus comes with all his holy ones' (1 Thessalonians 3:13).

The biblical principle, that the strength of our hope will determine the power of our incentive to live holy lives, cannot be disputed. Let us then set our hope fully on the grace to be given us when Jesus Christ is revealed (1 Peter 1:13) This world, to which we no longer belong (John 17:16), is heading for destruction. 'Since everything will be destroyed in this way, what kind of persons ought you to be?, asks Peter. 'You ought to live holy and godly lives as you look forward to the day of God and speed its coming' (2 Peter 3:11, 12). When the apostle says 'What kind of persons ought you to be?,' he is not really expecting an answer to his question. He expects us to know the answer. His statement is more like an exclamation.

Finally, do not miss Peter's surprising statement that the spiritual health of the Lord's people will determine, at least to some extent, the time of his coming. In other words, if we all live holy lives we speed the coming of the day of God! No doubt God, who knows the end from the beginning, also knows the day of Christ's coming, but this in no way lessens the importance of Peter's words. By our holy living, we may move the glorious day forward, and presumably, by our slackness and ill-discipline, retard it.

'When Christ, who is your life, appears, then you also will appear with him in glory. Put to death therefore, whatever belongs to your earthly nature: sexual immorality, impurity, lust, evil desires and greed, which is idolatry' (Colossians 3:4, 5).

CHAPTER TWELVE

When Perfection Comes

'When perfection comes, the imperfect disappears'
(1 Corinthians 13:10).

1. The Glorious Prospect

But nobody's perfect! So we say whenever we have cause to deplore
the blemishes on the character of someone who may otherwise be an
admirable person. And as with human beings, so with everything
else in this life. We may strive after perfection, but it eludes us.
Speaking for myself, almost all my life I have been dubbed a perfec-
tionist by my friends, and it has not always been intended as a
compliment. It is probably true, because whatever I do – paint a
picture, decorate a room, prepare a sermon, or write a book – I
suffer a sense of frustration with the finished product. For this
reason, I have often been advised to lower my standards, but even if
I were able to take the advice, I would still be unable to avoid the
frustration. Creation itself leaves us with a similar feeling. We
admire the breathtaking beauty and the astonishing complexity of it,
and for a fleeting moment we feel we are looking at perfection. But
then, when we remember it is all subject to decay and death, our
pleasure is tinged with sadness. This bondage to decay, according to
Paul, causes the whole creation to groan because it too is frustrated
(Romans 20-22).

The church suffers the same handicap. If we feel any concern
about the honour of our Lord's Name, it is inevitable that we shall
feel grieved by the church's imperfections. We long for the day when
she will be found to be 'without stain or wrinkle or any other
blemish' (Ephesians 5:27), but in the meantime we cannot escape

that feeling of frustration. As individual members we also feel the pain of our own imperfect contribution to the church's life and witness. It is said that if ever you find the perfect church, whatever else you do, do not join it, because you would spoil it!

In spite of all this, claims to sinless perfection in various forms have been made in the church throughout her history, and especially in later centuries by the various holiness movements that developed from the teaching of John Wesley. But sin, according to Wesley, was merely conscious transgression, and perfection therefore was freedom from conscious sin. But even on the basis of this watered-down definition of sin, the claim cannot be substantiated, and to think of ourselves as perfect can only be an extreme form of self-deception. According to the apostle John, any claim to perfection is a sin because it is a lie: 'If we claim to be without sin, we deceive ourselves and the truth is not in us' (1 John 1:8).

But the day is coming when everything that is imperfect will disappear altogether. Perfect holiness will put an end to striving. Perfect knowledge will put an end to teaching and learning. Perfect fellowship will put an end to bickering and division. Perfect happiness will put an end to sighing and groaning. A perfect body will put an end to pain. Perfect sight will put an end to those partial glimpses we have by faith. 'Now we see but a poor reflection; then we shall see face to face. Now I know in part; then I shall know fully, even as I am fully known' (1 Corinthians 13:12.). The words of David in surely one of the most thrilling verses in the entire Psalter, express the hope of every child of God: 'And I – in righteousness – I shall see your face; when I awake, I shall be satisfied with seeing your likeness' (Psalm 17:15). What a glorious prospect!

As we saw in chapter eight, the general idea of the word 'perfect' (Greek: teleios) as it is used in the New Testament, is that of completeness or maturity, reaching the point where all that is infantile or inadequate has been left behind. It may refer to being 'grown up' as a Christian, as in Ephesians 4:13, where the word is translated 'mature'. The apostle speaks of believers being built up 'until we all reach unity in the faith and in the knowledge of the Son of God and become mature...' But in other texts the word means 'perfect' as we normally understand the word – perfect in the sense of being faultless. In 1 Corinthians 13:10 it refers to the completion of God's work of grace in the glory to come when redeemed sinners will be free of all imperfections; 'but when perfection comes, the imperfect disappears.' In that day, creation 'will be liberated from its bondage to decay and brought into the glorious freedom of the children of God' (Romans 8:21).

2. Ever Increasing Glory

My wife and I were sitting on a wooden bench in total darkness and complete silence. Many other people were sitting behind us and on either side, but we could neither see them nor hear them. We were all peering into the intense darkness and listening very carefully. What a relief it was when we saw a tiny glow of light in the distance and heard the faint sound of music! As the music became louder and the light a little brighter, we were able to discern the faint outlines of three men in a boat playing violins. After a while, as the light became gradually brighter, we were all invited to get into small boats to be ferried across a lake. After disembarking, we walked through a long cave in subdued light, gradually emerging into the full light of the sun. We had to protect our eyes for a few minutes until they became accustomed to the bright light. Our memorable visit to the Caves of Drach on the island of Majorca was over.

To me, the experience was a graphic illustration of the believer's journey from spiritual darkness into the glorious light of God's presence, where there is no darkness at all. Christ, who is the light of the world (John 8:12) shines in the darkness (John 1:5) and all whom he chooses are called out of darkness into his wonderful light (1 Peter 2:9). At first, the light is but faint compared with the light of God's immediate presence, but it is as much as we can stand, especially after being so long in the darkness. And it is enough for our need. We understand that Jesus came into the world so that no one who believes in him should stay in darkness (John 12:46), and fixing our eyes on Jesus, we go forward in faith and obedience, seeing more and more of his marvellous light until at last faith gives way to sight. Then, we shall see Jesus perfectly, and be changed into his perfect likeness at once (1 John 3:2), and so 'we will be with the Lord for ever' (1 Thessalonians 4:17).

In the meantime, just as the Holy Spirit shined into our hearts to reveal Jesus to us when were called out of darkness, so he continues to do so in order to prepare us for the perfection to come. From the time of our conversion, all through our lives, the glory of God is revealed to us by faith in the person of the Lord Jesus Christ, and it is vitally important that as we grow older our vision of his glory should become clearer. We are 'predestined to be conformed to the image of his Son' (Romans 8:29), and the process must begin here.

Three distinct stages can be discerned in our emergence from the intense darkness of the Caves of Drach. First, we were sitting in total darkness in the underground cavern, unable to move because we could not see a thing. Then a glimmer of light began to shine and grew gradually brighter as we slowly emerged from the caves. Finally we came out of the gloom into the dazzling sunshine.

We see three similar stages in our emergence from spiritual darkness into the glory of heaven. First, by nature we were darkened in our understanding and separated from the life of God through the ignorance that was in us (Ephesians 4:18). We were incapable of understanding the things of God. They were foolishness to us, because the 'god of this age has blinded the minds of unbelievers, so that they cannot see the light of the gospel of the glory of Christ, who is the image of God.' Second, he 'made his light shine in our hearts to give us the light of the knowledge of the glory of God in the face of Christ' (2 Corinthians 4:4-6), so that we are now 'light in the Lord' (Ephesians 5:8). By using the words 'minds' and 'hearts' the apostle is not drawing a line between the intellect and the emotions as we might think. The two words are similar in meaning. He is thinking of the whole man; his reasoning powers, his emotions and his will. The light of the knowledge of Christ for the believer is in his mind and heart simultaneously; it is both knowledge and experience at the same time. As we grow in grace, the light increases, so that we are being transformed into Christ's likeness 'with ever increasing glory' (2 Corinthians 3:18). The final stage will be reached when we see Jesus face to face and are changed into his likeness. The gloom which prevents us from fully comprehending his glory now will be banished altogether. We shall know him perfectly, just as God knows us perfectly.

In the darkness of stage one we were unable to comprehend the glory of Christ revealed to us at stage two. And in stage two we are unable to comprehend his glory as it will be revealed at stage three. But the gap between stages two and three is much larger than it is between stage one and two. Our eyes adjusted gradually to the increasing light as we emerged from the caves, but when we came out into the blazing sunshine we had to shade them from the brilliance. If then we realise what a wonderful change has taken place in our lives since we were brought out of darkness, we should be looking forward with sheer delight to the much greater change when we see Jesus as he is. In that day, the darkness of our remaining ignorance will be finally and permanently removed. Once glorified, not a single shadow will remain to cloud our understanding. All who really love the light will yearn for that day.

3. The Fulness of Glory

A strange thing happened to me on a recent visit to Chatsworth House in Derbyshire. I had just emerged from the Gentlemen's toilets, to find myself confronted by two women who were total strangers to me. One of them asked if I would kindly go back into the toilets to make sure it was convenient for them to enter! A little perplexed, I did as requested and invited the two ladies in. After some conversation with them, I discovered that a disabled visitor had complained about the door on the new cubicles which opened inwards instead of outwards, making access in a wheel chair impossible. To my surprise, the older of the two ladies turned out to be the Duchess of Devonshire (Chatsworth House is the residence of the Duke and Duchess and is open to the public) who had come to see the problem for herself. She thanked me profusely for my help and I left. The Duchess was incognito of course, and there was nothing about her dress or manner that would have given me the slightest clue about her status.

There are people in this world however who are also incognito but have a much more noble status. They too have a title, not bought with money, but conferred on them freely by the highest authority in the universe. They are the children of God! 'How great,' says John, 'is the love the Father has lavished on us, that we should be called children of God. And this is what we are!' The apostle goes on to explain that 'The reason the world does not know us is that it did not know him' (1 John 3:1). Just as the glory of Christ was not recognised by those who had not received the precious gift of faith, so now the children of God are not recognised for the same reason. Our lives are 'hidden with Christ in God' (Colossians 3:3).

When it comes to our future glory however, even we do not know what we shall be like. 'We shall be like him,' says John, but exactly 'what we will be has not yet been made known' (1 John 3:2). I like the story of the queen of Sheba who, having heard of the fame of King Solomon, came to Jerusalem to see for herself. When she 'saw all the wisdom of Solomon and the palace he had built, the food on his table, the seating of his officials, the attending servants in their robes, his cupbearers, and the burnt offerings he made at the temple of the Lord, she was overwhelmed' She had never seen anything like it. 'She said to the king, "The report I heard in my own country about your achievement and your wisdom is true. But I did not believe these things until I came and saw with my own eyes. Indeed, not even half was told me…"' (1 Kings 10:4-7).

The glory of Jesus we are to see is not the glory of an earthly king, but the glory of the King of kings, seated at 'the right hand of the majesty in heaven' (Hebrews: 1:3) Commenting on the words of the Queen of Sheba, Matthew Henry says: 'Glorified saints...will say that it was a true report which they heard of the happiness of heaven, but that the thousandth part was not told them.' The Queen however, did not believe the reports of the glory of King Solomon, until she saw it with her own eyes. But we do believe the 'reports' of the glory of the King of Kings given to us in Scripture. Those who do not believe them will never see them.

The view we now have by faith of his glory is imperfect, variable, and confined. By contrast, our view of him by sight will be perfect, constant and substantial. We shall not only be given eyes to see him in all his perfection, but also the ability to appreciate his beauty. All the imperfections in our present view of him will be removed. For when perfection comes, the imperfect disappears. Further, when we see him, the sight will be suddenly and absolutely transforming. The steady growth into his likeness will be completed in an instant.

The idea of seeing Jesus forever may give the impression that heaven is a place where we shall have nothing to do but gaze on him. The verse of an old hymn may encourage this notion:

> Father of Jesus, love's reward,
> What rapture will it be,
> Prostrate before Thy throne to lie,
> And gaze and gaze on Thee!
> *Frederick William Faber (1814-63).*

But far from being merely spectators when the glory of Jesus is revealed, we are the people in whom the glory is revealed. It is a glory we shall share. 'I consider' says the apostle, 'that our present sufferings are not worth comparing with the glory that will be revealed in us' (Romans 8:18). It is foolish to speculate on the detail, but we can be sure that we shall have perfect freedom to worship God as we ought, and unrestricted opportunity for perfect fellowship that will be the source of endless and unfading joy. God's redeemed people living in God's renewed world will certainly not be idle.

4. Our Glorified Body

Two children, not more than ten years old, arrived at the vicarage with a cardboard box containing two skulls and three or four human bones. The children said they had found them on the surface of the ground in the church graveyard. I guessed at once what had happened. At the end of the churchyard the land fell away steeply to a field below. In this field, contractors were laying foundations for new houses. I had already complained that their excavations were too near the bottom of the slope, but no action had been taken. Now, a landslide had occurred and the bones of people long since dead were exposed to view. To be on the safe side, I reported the matter to the police who insisted that the bones be examined to determine their age. They were found to be well over a hundred years old, and were re-interred in another place.

When the Bible writers speak of the resurrection of the dead, they are not using symbolic language as so many think. They are talking about the raising to life of the corrupted bodies of all people, some of whom will have been dead for thousands of years. It is because this seems so incredible that many reject the idea. How, for example, will God be able to find the right bones of the people who were buried in that graveyard so long ago, now that they are buried in different places? Or, even worse, how will he reconstitute the bodies of those whose ashes have scattered over a wide area, or those who have been blown to bits? But the question not only betrays a failure to understand the power of God but a serious lack of faith as well – as if God, who created man from the dust of the ground and breathed life into him will have any difficulty!

Such scepticism is not new however; some people in the church at Corinth in the first century did not believe it either. Paul antici-pated their objections: 'But someone may ask, "How are the dead raised? With what kind of body do they come?" How foolish! What you sow does not come to life unless it dies. When you sow, you do not plant the body that will be, but just a seed, perhaps of corn or of something else. But God gives it a body as he has determined...' (1 Corinthians 15:35-38). In these timeless words, Paul is remind-ing us that God performs the miracle of re-creation under our noses every time a seed produces fruit. The fruit has the same nature as the seed, and yet it is different because the seed has disintegrated. Perhaps the best illustration of this process is the way potatoes grow. When we turn the soil over at harvest time, there among all the lovely new potatoes is the decayed mass of the seed potato we planted. It has died; but in the process God has given life to the new potatoes as he has determined. They have the same identity as the old potato, and yet they are different.

In the same passage, Paul goes on to point out that God has created all sorts of bodies – earthly bodies like human beings, animals, birds and fish, and heavenly bodies like the sun, moon and stars, all of which are designed to suit their own environment. He then draws a parallel with the resurrection of the dead: 'The body that is sown is perishable, it is raised imperishable. It is sown in dishonour, it is raised in glory; it is sown in weakness, it is raised in power; it is sown a natural body, it is raised a spiritual body' (1 Corinthians 15:42-44. The word 'spiritual' does not mean ethereal or immaterial, but a body adapted to our new spiritual nature in heaven). Our new body will be perfectly suited to our new environment.

To doubt God's word or his power (Matthew 22:29) is a wicked thing to do. God is able to raise the dead whatever the condition of their mortal remains, and we should not have the slightest doubt about it. The prophecy of Daniel tells us that 'Multitudes who sleep in the dust of the earth will awake: some to everlasting life, others to shame and everlasting contempt. Those who are wise will shine like the brightness of the heavens, and those who lead many to righteousness, like the stars for ever and ever' (Daniel 12:2, 3). The prophet's meaning is that God will raise all the dead, the righteous and the unrighteous, and reconstruct their bodies even though they are now nothing but dust.

The power of God to do this always impressed itself on my mind whenever I found myself scattering the ashes of a deceased person. Just recently I was asked to scatter the ashes of a sailor at sea. The mourners, most of them ex-sailors, hired a small fishing boat and we sailed for about an hour before switching off the engine. It was a windy day and the sea was rough. At the appropriate point in the short service, the urn holding the ashes was opened and as the ashes were poured out, the wind caught them and blew them in all directions, some coming back into my face!

Although our purpose here is to focus on the resurrection of believers in order to encourage them to look forward to that day when we shall see Jesus face to face, we should not forget what his appearing will mean for those who reject him. The Scriptures are very clear; the bodies of unbelievers will awake 'to shame and contempt' (See Daniel 12:2, 3 above) or, as John puts it, they will 'rise to be condemned' (John 5:29). The joy we feel because we have been delivered from this terrible destiny must always be tempered by a concern for those – friends and relatives among them – who are still unconverted.

Unless the Lord comes during our lifetime believers, like everyone else, must die. We share the penalty of sin in our bodies, which is death. But he who now dwells in our hearts will give life to our dead bodies and make them like Christ's glorious body (Philippians 3:21). 'And if the Spirit of him who raised Jesus from the dead is living in you,' says Paul, 'he who raised Christ from the dead will also give life to your mortal bodies through his Spirit, who lives in you' (Romans 8:11).

The teaching of some Greek philosophers that the human body is an evil prison from which our souls will one day be set free, contrasts sharply with the teaching of Scripture. The body of a believer, says Paul, is the temple of the Holy Spirit (1 Corinthians 6:19). A temple is a house of God; a building in which God dwells. Our bodies are temples because God the Holy Spirit lives in them and therefore they are to be used to glorify him, and that forever! The resurrection of our bodies will not change their purpose, but it will change their nature so that their purpose is perfectly realised. In the meantime, because our loathsome sinful nature is still very much alive in these dying bodies, the beauty of Jesus cannot be displayed in its fulness, but our resurrection bodies, freed from every taint of sin, will express it perfectly.

In addition, our bodies must be changed because 'flesh and blood cannot inherit the kingdom of God, nor does the perishable inherit the imperishable.' Mortals cannot enter heaven. Comparing Adam and Christ, Paul says: 'Just as we have borne the likeness of the earthly man so shall we bear the likeness of the man from heaven' (1 Corinthians 15:49, 50). Just as we have inherited a perishable body like Adam's, so shall we inherit an imperishable body like Christ's. Without this new body, no longer subject to pain or death (Revelation 21:4), our redemption cannot be complete. In our present bodies even we, 'who have the firstfruits of the Spirit, groan inwardly as we wait eagerly for our adoption as sons, the redemption of our bodies' (Romans 8:23). Although the groaning may not always be audible, we all know what a burden our mortal bodies are, prone to temptation and pain. If it were not so, we would not wait so eagerly for their redemption.

Under the Old Testament law, the first sheaf of grain harvested was to be brought to the priest. (Leviticus 23:10). It was known as the firstfruit. It was a promise of the harvest to come. Paul almost certainly had this in mind when he referred to the resurrection of the Lord Jesus Christ as 'the firstfruits of those who have fallen asleep' (1 Corinthians 15:20), for his resurrection is the guarantee of our resurrection. The same is true of Paul's words describing Christ as 'the firstborn from among the dead' (Colossians 1:18). By his resurrection, he became the first of millions who will be raised from the dead and take a new and glorious body. 'Listen, I tell you a mystery: We will not all sleep, but we will all be changed – in a flash, in the twinkling of an eye, at the last trumpet. For the trumpet will sound, the dead will be raised imperishable, and we will be changed. For the perishable must clothe itself with the imperishable, and the mortal with immortality' (1 Corinthians 15:51-53).

7. The Restoration of All Things

After the birth of their first child a number of women I know said, 'never again'. And yet, most of them went back on their word and willingly went through it again, some of them several times. Why? Because labour pains, unlike other pains, are not omens of death but of life, and therefore they are soon forgotten in the joy of a new birth. This is how we should see the anguish and frustration of the present order of things. In the poetic style of some of the Old Testament writers (who speak of the rivers clapping their hands and the mountains singing together for joy [Psalm 98:8; Isaiah 55:12]), Paul compares creation to a pregnant woman: The 'whole creation' he says, 'has been groaning, as in the pains of childbirth right up to the present time' (Romans 8:22). The pains of creation are not the prelude to death, but life – abundant life, everlasting life, perfect life. They are the birthpangs of a completely new order.

In the meantime there are many things to cause us anxiety about the future of our world – the threat of nuclear catastrophe, global warming, the population explosion, deforestation – to mention but a few. But the believer need not worry. The Lord Jesus Christ holds all things together (Colossians 1:17) and nothing can disintegrate except by his word. This does not mean that we may abandon our responsibility to look after the environment, but it does mean that we have no power to prevent the destruction of the world when God's time comes.

The world shares in the curse (Genesis 3:14-19), and therefore in its present state of decay it is not suitable for the glorified children of God to live in. It, like them, needs to be changed. Indeed, the Scripture teaches that creation cannot break free from its frustration until the children of God are glorified and revealed. The new world must wait for new people. Paul is explicit about this. One day creation itself will be 'liberated from its bondage to decay and brought into the glorious freedom of the children of God' (Romans 8:21). Jesus clearly had the new creation in mind when he spoke of 'the renewal of all things' (Matthew 19:28; see also Revelation 21:5). So did the apostle Peter when he said: 'He' (Christ) 'must remain in heaven until the time comes for God to restore everything, as he promised long ago through his holy prophets' (Acts 3:21). The dramatic manner in which the earth will be changed when the Lord returns is briefly described in Peter's second letter: 'That day will bring about the destruction of the heavens by fire, and the elements will melt in the heat. But in keeping with his promise we are looking forward to a new heaven and a new earth, the home of righteousness' (2 Peter 3:12, 13). In this nuclear age, Peter's words have taken on a new significance. His description of the destruction of this earth sounds astonishingly like a nuclear explosion. We cannot say for certain what fire means, but at least, Peter's words are now taken more seriously than they used to be.

Once the earth is purged by fire, the redeemed children of God shall enjoy the delights of a new heaven and a new earth filled with the glory of God. We shall walk the streets in safety because there will be no muggers, no pickpockets, no handbag-snatchers, no drunken drivers. We shall have no need of insurance policies because there will be no burglars, arsonists or natural disasters. We shall have no need of doctors because we shall never be sick. We shall have no weapons because there will be no wars. We shall not have to muzzle the dog because it will not bite. There will be no more funerals, cemeteries or crematoria because there will be no death. There will be no policemen, no law courts and no prisons, because no one will do wrong. We shall have no fear because there will be nothing to be afraid of. We shall inhabit the promised land at last, the new Jerusalem to which Abraham was looking forward so long ago, 'the city with foundations, whose architect and builder is God' (Hebrews 11:10; see also Genesis 17:8).

The Old Testament prophets had a lot to say about this wonderful new earth. 'The desert and the parched land will be glad; the wilderness will rejoice and blossom. Like the crocus it will burst into bloom; it will rejoice greatly and shout for joy' (Isaiah 35:1-2). 'The wolf will live with the lamb, the leopard will lie down with the goat, the calf and the lion and the yearling together; and a little child will lead them. The cow will feed with the bear, their young will lie down together, and the lion will eat straw like the ox. The infant will play near the hole of the cobra, and the young child put his hand into the viper's nest. They will neither harm nor destroy on all my holy mountain, for the earth will be full of the knowledge of the LORD as the waters cover the sea' (Isaiah 11:6-9).

John's vision in Revelation 21 adds more colour to the picture: 'Then I saw a new heaven and a new earth, for the first heaven and the first earth had passed away, and there was no longer any sea. I saw the Holy City, the new Jerusalem, coming down out of heaven from God, as a bride beautifully dressed for her husband. And I heard a loud voice from the throne saying: "Now the dwelling of God is with men, and he will live with them. They will be his people, and God himself will be with them and be their God. He will wipe every tear from their eyes. There will be no more death or mourning or crying or pain, for the old order of things has passed away"' (Verses 1-4). Although John describes everything as 'new', we must not take this to mean there will be no continuity (The Greek word is *kainos* which means freshness, and not *neos* which means recently created). Heaven and earth will be 'new' in the sense that the purifying fire will remove every trace of the curse. There will be no weeds, no rust or rot, no hard labour (Genesis 3:17-19). John describes the holy city as the 'new' Jerusalem to distinguish her from the present city. And he calls the city 'holy' because there will be no more sin to spoil her beauty. Her continuity with the church is seen in the fulfilment of the great covenant promise: 'They will be his people, and God himself will be with them and be their God.' This is the promise that goes back to the time of Abraham, and is repeated again and again throughout the Bible (Genesis 17:7, 8; Jeremiah 24:7; 2 Corinthians 6:16, and many other places). The final fulfilment of this promise will mean complete redemption for the church. She will be a perfect church, in perfect communion with her God; a church no longer divided by time, space, or disagreement. What is true of believers and their glorified bodies is therefore also true of the new earth and the new church: just as we as individuals will be recognisable as the same people, so the earth will be recognisable as the same earth, and the church as the same church.

But it is not the perfect earth, nor the perfect church that fills our hearts with delight so much as the glory and beauty of our beloved Lord. Further on in John's vision an angel said to him: 'Come, I will show you the bride, the wife of the Lamb.' Then, says John, the angel 'carried me away in the Spirit to a mountain great and high, and showed me the Holy City, Jerusalem, coming down out of heaven from God. It shone with the glory of God, and its brilliance was like that of a very precious jewel, like a jasper, clear as crystal…' (Revelation 21:9-11). The bride of the Lamb and the Holy City both stand for the renewed church, as we have just seen. But now we see why the church is so radiant, shining with the glory of God. It is because she is married to the Lamb, the Lord Jesus Christ. It is to him and him alone that we owe our future glory. It is because of the church's union with him that God's glory will shine through her. The marriage we mentioned in the last chapter (Revelation 19:6-8) has now taken place, and the Lord Jesus Christ has presented the church to himself as 'a radiant church, without stain or wrinkle or any other blemish' (Ephesians 5:26). 'Hallelujah! For our Lord God

Almighty reigns. Let us rejoice and be glad and give him the glory! For the wedding of the Lamb has come, and his bride has made herself ready.' The long separation is over and the eternal celebrations now begin!

This then is the glory we now contemplate by faith – a world of breathtaking beauty in which nothing is temporary, nothing is displeasing, and from which God's judgment has effectively removed everything that spoils – and a church in perfect harmony, in which nothing spoils our fellowship with God and with each other. But more than that, it is the glory of Jesus our Saviour and Friend. Nothing in this world can thrill the soul like the prospect of seeing him with our own eyes.

In view of our glorious future, how can we allow ourselves to be preoccupied with the vain pursuits of worldly men? How can we live as if we were in this world forever? How can we apply our minds to our secular interests day after day, week after week, and never turn our minds to the glory to come? This is not the attitude of people who are predestined to be like Jesus. We should rejoice in this, that one day soon, faith will give way to sight and we shall 'be with the Lord for ever' (1 Thessalonians 4:17).

6. After Death, What?

Some believers are anxious about what happens between death and the coming of the Lord. One of the reasons for this is that Paul refers to the death of believers as 'sleep' (1 Corinthians 15:20), which may give the impression that those who die are not conscious. Support for this view is supposed to be found in the Old Testament where death is sometimes spoken of as unconsciousness; Psalm 6:5 for example: 'No one remembers you when he is dead. Who praises you from the grave?' And since God will not judge us until Christ returns, how can we enter into conscious joy before that day?

The theory is mistaken. Paul refers to the death of the body as sleep because none of the terrors of death can afflict the believer. Death is like going to bed as usual and waking up in a different place. As for the supposed need to wait for God's verdict on judgement day, God has already given his promise that there is 'no condemnation for those who are in Christ Jesus' (Romans 8:1). Along with everyone else, we must 'appear before the judgment seat of Christ, that each one may receive what is due to him for the things done while in the body, whether good or bad' (2 Corinthians 5:10). But since Christ has already made atonement for all our sins, past, present and future, there can be no question of condemnation. The judgment of unbelievers will be based on divine justice so that their punishment will be what they deserve. The judgment of believers will be based on grace, so that they will not get the punishment they deserve. Nevertheless – and this is very important – their deeds will be taken into account so that the honour conferred on them will be in the nature of a reward. Paul makes this very clear in 1 Corinthians 3:13-15. Speaking of the quality of each Christian's work, he says: '...the Day will bring it to light. It will be revealed with fire, and the fire will test the quality of each man's work. If what he has built survives, he will receive his reward. If it is burned up, he will suffer loss; he himself will be saved, but only as one escaping through the flames.'

To come back to the point, many texts of Scripture prove that the believer is conscious after death. What sense would the words of Jesus to the dying thief make if this were not the case: 'Today you will be with me in paradise' (Luke 23:43)? And how could Paul claim that 'to depart and be with Christ...is better by far' (Philippians 1:23) if he was not going to be awake to enjoy him? Yet for some, the anxiety is still not relieved. They still wonder how it can be far better to be with Christ when we have not yet received our resurrection bodies. How can we enjoy his presence when we do not have the means to communicate with him? In 2 Corinthians 5:1-5, Paul agrees that to have 'naked' souls is not an attractive idea, but goes on to reveal to us that immediately after death we shall be clothed with our heavenly dwelling. These are the apostle's words: 'Now we know that if the earthly tent we live in is destroyed, we have a building from God, an eternal house in heaven, not built by human hands. Meanwhile we groan, longing to be clothed with our heavenly dwelling, because when we are clothed we will not be found naked. For while we are in this tent, we groan and are burdened, because we do not wish to be unclothed but to be clothed with our heavenly dwelling, so that what is mortal may be swallowed up by life.'

It is not easy to say what 'our heavenly dwelling' is. It is presented to us as a building and a garment. We know Paul cannot be talking about our resurrection bodies because they will not be raised until the Lord returns. And yet, he says that our heavenly dwelling is 'an eternal house in heaven,' a place we shall inhabit forever. This brings our Lord's words to mind again: 'In my Father's house are many rooms; if it were not so, I would have told you. I am going there to prepare a place for you' (John 14:2). Admittedly, many questions are left open to which we would love to know the answer, but we shall have to be patient. Surely, enough is revealed to assure us that we shall be with Jesus immediately after death and that we shall not be bodiless spirits. We shall find it far better than groaning in a decaying body in a decaying world.

> 'Oh, the depth of the riches of the wisdom and
>   knowledge of God!
> How unsearchable his judgments, and his paths
>   beyond tracing out!
> "Who has known the mind of the Lord?
> Or who has been his counsellor?"...
> For from him and through him and to him are all
>   things.
> To him be the glory for ever! Amen'
>   (Romans 11:33-36).

Epilogue

Some practical advice may be helpful, but if you are looking for new ideas, better methods, or quick fixes for our spiritual maladies, you will not find them here. The remedy is as old as the problem, and it will not be found anywhere except in the Scriptures. What we all need in the present crisis is to seek for the grace and strength to apply it.

First of all, we must get our priorities right. Wrong priorities are the cause of many spiritual ills. One of the tutors at the theological college where I trained for the ministry, advised the students not to get involved in emotional relationships with the opposite sex because it would be a serious hindrance to study. Some of the younger men found the advice rather difficult to follow. One young man fell madly in love with a girl he had met briefly at the University Christian Union. His feeling for her was so intense it affected his sleep, his appetite and, of course, his studies!

We can hardly blame the young man for going against the advice of his tutor, but the story does illustrate the powerful attraction of the world when we try to set our minds on things above (Colossians 3:1). When it comes to the discipline of turning the heart heavenwards, there is always something competing for our affections, and probably something quite legitimate. This is the reason so many of us find the daily discipline of Bible-study and prayer so difficult. Even when we set time aside for the purpose, our minds are so occupied with worldly affairs we derive little benefit.

The trouble is that few of us stop to ask ourselves why this happens; and why our minds do not wander anything like as much when we apply them to our worldly interests. A little self-examination would quickly show that the reason lies in the fact that we put a higher value on the things of this world than we do on the 'things above'. It is primarily a question of priority. We appear to have forgotten where our real interests lie, with the result that we are more concerned to build a bigger bank balance than to live for the glory of Christ.

Jesus warned us about this very thing: 'Do not store up for yourselves treasures on earth, where moth and rust destroy, and where thieves break in and steal. But store up for yourselves treasures in heaven, where moth and rust do not destroy, and where thieves do not break in and steal. For where your treasure is, there your heart will be also' (Matthew 6:19-21). Jesus was not saying that we should be financially irresponsible or give all our money away and live as paupers. He was warning us against trying to serve God and money at the same time. It simply cannot be done. Either one or the other will take priority. 'No man can serve two masters. Either he will hate the one and love the other, or he will be devoted to the one and despise the other. You cannot serve both God and Money' (Matthew 6:24). We have a very similar command in John 6:27: 'Do not work for food that spoils, but for food that endures to eternal life, which the Son of Man will give you.' Here again Jesus is not saying we should not work for a living, but that food for the soul is far more important than food for the body. The broad road to destruction is well worn by the feet of those who love lawful things more than Christ.

I once asked an eighty-year-old friend of mine why the apostle Paul had a stronger desire to be with Christ than most of us have today. She thought it was because Paul did not have a wife and family to provide for and none of the comforts of life that we enjoy. He suffered privation and distress and his life was often under threat. That there is some truth in this I do not doubt, but it is certainly not the whole truth. There is simply no comparison between this life, no matter how good it is, and the glory to come, and in any case, we are not here for long. Is it not much more likely that the reason for Paul's confidence was that he had his priorities right? It is not possible to read his letters without being impressed by the importance he attaches to eternal things, and his strong assurance of eternal life was undoubtedly the fruit of this. His desire to depart and be with Christ therefore, was not a form of escapism. How could it be when it was counterbalanced by an equally strong longing to remain in the world and to engage in more 'fruitful labour' for the Lord? 'Yet what shall I choose?' he asks himself, 'I do not know' (Philippians 1:22-24). What a difference it would make in our lives if we had the same dilemma! Many of us are filled with more dread than delight at the thought of leaving this world to be with Christ, and heaven is too often seen as the place to which we must go when it is no longer possible to stay here.

Well would it be for us if, like Paul, our desire to remain here arose out of a desire to serve the Lord, and to press on to win the prize for which God has called us heavenwards in Christ Jesus (Philippians 3:14). But godly discontentment with spiritual attainments is a rare thing today. And yet only those who experience it will make progress. Contentment with our income or our status in life is 'great gain' (1 Timothy 6:6), but contentment with our spiritual attainment is a great loss. It not only betrays a slothful attitude towards heavenly things, but shows contempt for God's promises – promises that are given to encourage us to make progress towards our goal (Hebrews 6:17, 18). We know only too well that it is not easy to maintain a heavenly frame of mind when the appeal of affluence and materialism is never far from our sight.

Secondly, we must realise afresh that we are called to holiness. We have a solemn obligation to our gracious God to grow in the likeness of Christ. We must understand that holiness is an indispensable preparation for the glory to come and therefore nothing must have a higher priority. 'Just as he who called you is holy, so be holy in all you do; for it is written, "Be holy, because I am holy"' (1 Peter 1:15, 16). Practically, it will mean attending carefully to the means of grace – to teaching, worship, fellowship and prayer, as well as to our private devotions. It will mean that we no longer conform to the pattern of this world (Romans 12:2) but rather that we set our hearts on things above where Christ is seated at the right hand of God (Colossians 3:1-4). And as with everything else in the Christian life, it will involve effort. Not that we have power to achieve it on our own. 'Our competence comes from God' (2 Corinthians 3:5).

Many years ago, before the days of windscreen heaters, I had to make a journey from Manchester to Southport in thick fog. The conditions were so bad that I could not see the opposite side of the road. Just when I was beginning to feel the task was impossible, I realised that the inside of the windscreen had misted up. When I cleaned it, visibility improved immediately and I was able to make headway. In a similar way, trials of various kinds may impair our view of Christ, and there is nothing we can do about them. But how easy it is to forget that there may be mist on the inside of the glass, caused by our disobedience, sloth and the like. In this case, there is something we can do about it, and do it we must.

Believers who are in the regular habit of meditating on the glory of Christ are much more likely to notice when the mist is on the inside, because they will be much more sensitive to the sins that cause it. As we see him more clearly, we learn to love him more dearly and that will show itself by a willingness to do what he says (John 14:15). And we shall find it increasingly difficult to settle for anything in our lives that displeases him. But if, on the other hand, we come to terms with just one sin, on the ground that it is a pleasure we cannot live without, or that it is no longer considered to be serious in today's society, our progress in holy living will come to a halt, and the joyful anticipation of the glory to come will be lost.

Thirdly, we need to recover an awareness of who we are. The other day I watched a screenplay on television on the early life of Queen Victoria. According to the play, Baroness Lehzen, young

Victoria's German governess, was in the habit of saying to the young heir to the throne: 'Remember who you are.' On one occasion during the play, the young princess turned to the baroness and said, 'I find it very hard to remember who I am.' Many believers suffer the same inability. The sheer delight of being 'heirs of God and co-heirs with Christ' (Romans 8:17) has been lost.

We also tend to be forgetful about our real and permanent assets – an inheritance in heaven that is worth more than all the silver and the gold in the world. When I was in the retail jewellery business it was not uncommon for customers to leave expensive jewellery for repair and then forget to collect it. I understand the same is true of banks. Millions of pounds have been deposited in accounts and then forgotten. Even valuables left in deposit boxes are never claimed. If the owners are of sound mind, we can only conclude their possessions did not mean much to them. Let us make sure we do not make the same mistake when it comes to our treasure in heaven.

Finally, nothing will be achieved unless we come back to the Bible. A keen awareness of our status and privileges as the children of God cannot be achieved any other way. If we are to know Christ the living Word better, we must know the written word better. We must crave the 'pure spiritual milk' of the word, so that by it we may grow up in our salvation (1 Peter 2:2, 3). As mother's milk is the right nourishment for new-born infants, so the word of God is the right food for born-again believers. And it must be taken daily so that the word of Christ begins to dwell in us richly (Colossians 3:16).

We may not be thrilled every time we read the word, but the times when we feel overwhelmed with joy because of what God has done are reserved for those who make it a habit. The scarcity of such foretastes of heaven in our lives is commonly due to neglect of God's word. It may well be therefore, that before we find Bible-study a delight, we shall have to see it first as a duty. The practice of the early church is an example to us in this matter. 'They devoted themselves to the apostles' teaching and to the fellowship, to the breaking of bread and to prayer' (Acts 2:42).

When we determine to give time to the word and to prayer, Satan will suggest a thousand and one reasons why we should be doing something else. And if we persist, he will drop the hint that there's nothing to be gained or that we are not competent to understand. But it is not a matter of competence but of God-given understanding (1 Corinthians 2:12, 14). God's people, with God's help, are capable of understanding much more than we realise.

Finally, a good test of our spiritual health is to ask ourselves a simple question: 'What do we think about in our quiet moments, when there is no external stimulus?' After being obliged to turn our minds to secular things for much of the day, what thoughts come to mind when it's all over? We may have thoughts of Christ when we are in church listening to a sermon, but where do our minds turn when they are free to go where they like? If they do not turn naturally and regularly to thoughts of Christ and the great salvation he has purchased for us, we may safely conclude that something is wrong. If, on the other hand, our minds are accustomed to meditating on the glory of Christ, they will return to him like a boomerang as soon as they have the opportunity. 'Who is wise? He will realise these things. Who is discerning? He will understand them' (Hosea 14:9).

> 'Glorify the LORD with me; let us exalt his name
>   together.
> Those who look to him are radiant;
> Their faces are never covered with shame'
>   (Psalm 34:3, 5).

The eclipse of the gospel

The creeping shadows of an eclipse are a symbol of the spiritual darkness that is slowly spreading across much of the Western world. Millions are walking in darkness but thankfully the light still shines here and there, stubbonly resisting the enveloping gloom.

The aim of this book is to challenge those who have departed from the Bible; to encourage those who believe it to be much more serious in their study of it; and to help those who teach others to come to a better understanding of it, whether they are full-time ministers or 'laymen'.

The eclipse of the gospel, Frank Allred, 224pp, 946462 63 1